Everywhere I go, I find that a poet has been there before me.

Sigmund Freud

For Belinda: who listened, advised and enthused
from the beginning

Bracelet of Bright Hair

A Year of Reading Poetry

Frances Thomas

With illustrations by the author

Published 2012 by arima publishing
www.arimapublishing.com

ISBN 978 1 84549 541 1

Printed and bound in the United Kingdom

Typeset in Garamond 12/16

arima publishing

ASK House, Northgate Avenue
Bury St Edmunds, Suffolk IP32 6BB
t: (+44) 01284 700321
www.arimapublishing.com

Introduction

This is the record of a year, 2010 to be precise, and the resolution I made at the start of that year. New Year Resolutions, with their in-built failure and potential for guilt don't work for me; from a lifetime of wrestling with it, I know my will power's not up to much, so it had to be a different kind of resolution. The *Guardian* website gave me the idea at the beginning of January. There is a weekly poem, and that week, it was Hardy's *The Darkling Thrush*. I decided that that was to be my task – a new poem, read with attention, as near to every day as I could.

As a teenager I read poetry both for pleasure and to show off. I remember slouching through school corridors with the yellow-covered *Penguin Book Of Contemporary Verse* stuffed into my blazer pocket, hoping it would annoy the nuns. I didn't understand everything I read, but often I just loved the way words lay on a page: *The only emperor is the Emperor of ice-cream...* What was all that about? Never mind; I liked its queer and special sounds. Later, I read English at University, and poetry turned into Duty. But there were also thrilling new worlds to explore – Anglo-Saxon, medieval poetry. There were poets I liked, and poets I didn't. Marvell was my favourite then, with his cool green gardens and glowing orange trees. I wasn't too keen on Wordsworth and I definitely didn't like Hardy.

I still went on – after a fashion – reading, and buying poetry. But then as the years went on, the necessity for reading poetry seemed to fade. Soon it started to feel like an indulgence. The poetry-shaped hole in the day shrank to a pinprick. It was either too early in the day, too afternoon-ish, and then, too late, to pick up a poetry book and just read. Other tasks called out with louder and more clamorous voices. The poetry books on the shelves grew just a little dusty, acquired the yellowish stiffness of unread, unnoticed books. I meant to get back into the habit, but somehow I didn't.

But when you feel there is an obligation upon you, that's different. After a few days, choosing my daily poem became essential, before the rest of the day could begin. Then I started jotting down a few notes. Then the writing turned into a sort of journal; I started looking for poems that suited my mood, or the things that were happening around me. The poems and the days were becoming bound up in each other in ways I hadn't imagined at the start of all this. And I realised that poetry – often just half-remembered scraps, or single lines, or just the recollection of a mood expressed in a poem, was far more deeply embedded in my consciousness than I'd ever realised. Poetry was simply part of my life, even if I'd sometimes forgotten it was there.

I made up some rules – there had to be rules, but I gave myself the choice of breaking them. Some days the poem was a random choice – eyes closed, picking blind from the poetry shelf, then opening the book, also at random. Only I decided not to do that every day because I knew I'd cheat. So I might chose a poem I half remembered but wanted to remember better; other days, a deliberate selection of poet, or poetry book; perhaps a first line that made me want to read on, or a title, or a metaphor that jumped out. Sometimes it was a poem related to the day, or what was in the paper, or what was going on around me. Sometimes I Googled through one of the many poetry sites online. Sometimes I just chose a poem for no reason. As the year went on, I started to ask friends and acquaintances to suggest poems. Their choices have surprised and delighted me.

Often, at the beginning of a week, I've wondered where to go for the next poem; even thought I'd run out of inspiration, didn't know where to look next. And then, somehow, magically, the poem arrived, as though it had flown in through my open window and landed on the kitchen table with a joyful flap of wings. And maybe that poem led on to another, and another, a trail of images and words and ideas. I've rediscovered old poems from my childhood, found entirely new ones by writers I'd never heard of. I never thought, at the beginning of the year, that I'd be writing a journal – I'm not a journal kind of person, but somehow I was, and somehow I did.

This isn't an anthology, – I wouldn't know how to start on an anthology. This journal hasn't even got all my favourite poems or poets in it. Some poets I adore and revere are absent from its pages. Copyright, which can be a tricky and tortuous matter, has something to do with it, but often it's just that other poems, that day, simply called out more loudly.

So here it is – a 'bracelet of bright hair' – and I hope you'll excuse the inadequacies of its collector, and read these poems with something of the excitement and delight with which I read them. I hope it will remind you of poems you once knew and have half forgotten, or take you back to poems deeply embedded in your own memories, or to poems that are always enmeshed with a particular experience. I hope it will introduce you to new and beautiful things, and poets you didn't know about. I hope it'll send you rushing back to your own poetry books. I hope, even, you'll disagree with some of my choices and mentally substitute your own. I hope this book might end up on your bedside table, and acquire several untidy bits of paper as bookmarks and the ringmarks of several coffee cups. I hope you read it. I hope you like it.

January

January 1ˢᵗ

This is the poem that started it all, and what a good way to begin. The change of year used to be exciting, a sense of anticipation along with the new date at the top of the schoolbook page, peering into the future; things were getting better and more interesting all the time. Once I even wrote a little poem to celebrate the New Year. I remember it started:

> *Goodbye, Fifty-one*
> *In you we've had lots of fun*
> *Welcome, welcome Fifty-two…*

(Well, I *was* only eight.)

But now, in my mid-sixties, hurtling towards my seventies, what do I feel? Not gloom exactly, though the world doesn't seem to become a nicer place with each passing year. Not depression, or dejection; oddly, those moods belong to youth, with its high impossible hopes and unachievable expectations. There's a sort of exultation to find yourself still here and everything still in place. But trepidation, too, as you know that inevitably one day your luck will run out. There's only one place to go, in the end.

So this poem, with its wintery pessimism, yet faint note of joy, suits well. And Hardy? Well, I like him now, at least his poems. Wild horses will never get me to read *Jude the Obscure* again. But then, I don't have to. That's one of the good things about being old. *Welcome, welcome, two thousand and ten….*

The gloom of Winter has seldom been better realised than in this poem – even the frost is grey rather than sparkling. 'Dregs' and 'desolate' beat like melancholy drums, and the bine-stems 'score' is only broken music. Hardy's use of odd, slightly archaic words, or made-up words , illimited, outleant, fervourless, beruffled, add to the strange, almost biblical atmosphere. Those words 'frail, gaunt and small' are deeply moving, although in reality Hardy probably couldn't have known whether or not the thrush was 'aged' or 'gaunt'. The ending doesn't bring comfort – there's no sense that the thrush's lyrical outpouring is going to lift Hardy's wintery pessimism.

The *Guardian* had much to say about the word 'darkling'. The dictionary meaning is simply 'in the dark' or 'obscure'. And yet the word, much loved by poets, seems to have a deeper resonance. One writer suggested it was more an equivalent of the German 'dunkeln' – becoming dark – and it does seem to have the suggestion of a deepening twilight, rather than utter darkness. Hardy seems to be describing the brief time when colours fade into greyness. Keats also listened 'darkling' to the joyful, mesmeric song of the nightingale.

The Darkling Thrush   Thomas Hardy

I leant upon a coppice gate
When Frost was spectre-grey,
And Winter's dregs made desolate
The weakening eye of day.
The tangled bine-stems scored the sky
Like strings of broken lyres,

And all mankind that haunted nigh
Had sought their household fires.

The land's sharp features seemed to be
The Century's corpse outleant,
His crypt the cloudy canopy,
The wind his death-lament.
The ancient pulse of germ and birth
Was shrunken hard and dry,
And every spirit upon earth
Seemed fervourless as I.

At once a voice arose among
The bleak twigs overhead
In a full-hearted evensong
Of joy illimited;
An aged thrush, frail, gaunt, and small,
In blast-beruffled plume,
Had chosen thus to fling his soul
Upon the growing gloom.

So little cause for carolings
Of such ecstatic sound
Was written on terrestrial things
Afar or nigh around,
That I could think there trembled through
His happy good-night air
Some blessed Hope, whereof he knew
And I was unaware.

January 6th

We drive through Dymock, a pretty Gloucestershire village every time we go to London, and I always think of Edward Thomas, but realise now how little I know about him, except that he was killed in the first World War. The most surprising discovery is that all his poems were produced in just two years, between late 1914 and 1917 when he was killed in France.

Though his family were Welsh, he was born in South London and went to school in Battersea. Later he lived in Kent and Hampshire. He was astonishingly handsome, more so, if his photo is to be believed, than Rupert Brooke; a long intense face with classically clean features and artistic flop of fair hair. He married young and worked for many years writing prose, to support himself and his family. Self doubt and crippling depression darkened his life. It was a meeting and then a friendship with Robert Frost , who lived in Dymock for a while, that gave him the confidence and sense of entitlement to start writing poetry in his 37th year. He joined the Artist's Rifles in 1915 –though he didn't have to join up then, and can no longer have felt the bounding idealism that led so many to join in 1914. He seems to have been escaping – himself, or the demons that shadowed him, and which are glimpsed in many of his poems:

And yet I still am half in love with pain,
With what is imperfect, with both tears and mirth,
With things that have an end, with life and earth,
And this moon that leaves me dark within the door.

(What a great title those last four words would make)

He's been associated with the Georgian movement and his reputation has suffered because of this. True, his poems often start on a gentle pastoral note, but read on, and the air darkens. *All I could lose, I lost*, he says and the reader isn't quite sure whether the 'loss' is spiritual ecstasy, or a deeper, darker loss, as he falls into the universe around him as into a black hole. The child's words that 'raise the dead' are ambiguous too; are the man and the child really the first people to impose history on this particular landscape? Were horse and rider ever here, ever dead? The poem is at once soothing, but disturbing.

The Brook   Edward Thomas

Seated once by a brook, watching a child
Chiefly that paddled, I was thus beguiled.
Mellow the blackbird sang and sharp the thrush
Not far off in oak and hazel brush,
Unseen. There was a scent like honeycomb
From mugwort dull. And down upon the dome
Of the stone the cart-horse kicks against so oft
A butterfly alighted. From aloft
He took the heat of the sun, and from below.
On the hot stone he perched contented so,
As if never a cart would pass again
That way; as if I were the last of men
And he the first of insects to have earth
And sun together and to know their worth.
I was divided between him and the gleam,
The motion, and the voices, of the stream,

The waters running frizzled over gravel,
That never vanish and for ever travel.
A grey flycatcher silent on a fence
And I sat as if we had been there since
The horseman and the horse lying beneath
The fir-tree-covered barrow on the heath,
The horseman and the horse with silver shoes,
Galloped the downs last. All that I could lose
I lost. And then the child's voice raised the dead.
'No one's been here before' was what she said
And what I felt, yet never should have found
A word for, while I gathered sight and sound.

January 8th

This is a case of the poem winning out over prejudice. My book fell open on *Hurrahing in Harvest* by Gerard Manley Hopkins. I'd thought of Hopkins as a poet one reads in word-drunk adolescence; if anyone had asked me recently, I'd have said that what I like of him now are the early, austere poems, before Sprung Rhythm and strange syntax had carried him off. I remember a discussion in school about the phrase from *The Habit of Perfection* - *Oh feel-of-primrose-hands…* and how it made us rub our hands together feeling uncomfortably clammy. I decided I wasn't going to like *Hurrahing in Harvest* and seeing the rhymes of *Saviour/ behaviour/ gave you/ a/* increased my resolve. I read the poem through a couple of times, and still didn't like it.

It was the word 'barbarous' catching my eye that suddenly worked like a time-release medicine. Colours suddenly flooded in, and the rhythms, heroic and exhilarating, began to work in my brain. The poem left me happy – hurrahing, in fact

Hurrahing in Harvest   Gerard Manley Hopkins

Summer ends now; now, barbarous in beauty, the stooks arise
Around; up above, what wind-walks! What lovely behaviour
Of silk-sack clouds! has wilder, wilful-wavier
Meal-drift moulded ever and melted across skies?

I walk, I lift up, I lift up heart, eyes,
Down all that glory in the heavens to glean our Saviour;
And, éyes, heárt, what looks, what lips yet gave you a
Rapturous love's greeting of realer, of rounder replies?

And the azurous hung hills are his world-wielding shoulder
Majestic—as a stallion stalwart, very-violet-sweet!—
These things, these things were here and but the beholder
Wanting; which two when they once meet,
The heart rears wings bold and bolder
And hurls for him, O half hurls earth for him off under his feet.

January 13th

I chose this because I was struggling to remember the last lines . (*der der der der… wild surmise, Silent upon a peak in Darien…*) It's a poem I read – or rather studied dutifully - in the sixth form and have hardly read since; a poem that you tend not to revisit simply because it's so well known. But nevertheless an experience you'd like to have now for the first time; so like stout Cortez, you could just gasp with wonder.

Only it wasn't stout Cortez who discovered the Pacific – it was stout Balboa. Here's the passage that Keats read, and then so magically misremembered, from Robertson's *History Of America:*

As soon as he beheld the Southern sea, stretching in endless prospect before him, he fell on his knees and lifting his hands to heaven returned thanks to God who had conducted him to a discovery so beneficial to his country and so honourable to himself. His followers, observing his transports, rushed forward to join in his wonder, exultation and gratitude.

Keats's friend Clarke describes the night the two had spent at Clarke's house in Clerkenwell, devouring Chapman's translation of the Odyssey. Clarke remembers how one line in particular had seized Keats's attention; describing a shipwrecked Ulysses coming out of the sea, dripping wet, Chapman wrote ; *The sea had soak'd his heart through.* At dawn, Keats hurried back to his lodgings in Dean Street, Southwark (now under London Bridge Station) and there, his pen rushing over the paper, he dashed off this sonnet. There were a just a couple of minor alterations to come, but the excitement he felt then still surges through the poem.

On First Looking in to Chapman's Homer   John Keats

Much have I travell'd in the realms of gold,
    And many goodly states and kingdoms seen;
    Round many western islands have I been
Which bards in fealty to Apollo hold.
Oft of one wide expanse had I been told,
    That deep-brow'd Homer ruled as his demesne:

Yet did I never breathe its pure serene
Till I heard Chapman speak out loud and bold:
Then felt I like some watcher of the skies
When a new planet swims into his ken;
Or like stout Cortez when with eagle eyes
He stared at the Pacific – and all his men
Look'd at each other with a wild surmise-
Silent, upon a peak in Darien.

January 19th

The day starts badly with a long spell of computer frustration. Something won't work, and the harder I try, the worse it gets and in the end my broadband packs up completely. I'm in a filthy mood. Like Manny in *Black Books* I need to swallow *The Little Book of Calm* before I can surface again.

So instead, I look for calmness in a poem. George Herbert is the calmest poet I know, and though his rage certainly wasn't directed at a computer, the poem suits as he works through anger (*collar* and *choler* – a seventeenth century pun) indignation and disobedience, finally to subside in a mood of serene resignation.

And then, eventually, magically, my broadband reconnects itself.

The Collar   George Herbert

I struck the board, and cried, "No more;
I will abroad!
What? shall I ever sigh and pine?
My lines and life are free, free as the road,
Loose as the wind, as large as store.

Shall I be still in suit?
Have I no harvest but a thorn
To let me blood, and not restore
What I have lost with cordial fruit?
 Sure there was wine
Before my sighs did dry it; there was corn
Before my tears did drown it.
 Is the year only lost to me?
Have I no bays to crown it,
No flowers, no garlands gay? All blasted?
 All wasted?
Not so, my heart; but there is fruit,
 And thou hast hands.
Recover all thy sigh-blown age
On double pleasures: leave thy cold dispute
Of what is fit and not. Forsake thy cage,
 Thy rope of sands,
Which petty thoughts have made, and made to thee
Good cable, to enforce and draw,
 And be thy law,
While thou didst wink and wouldst not see.
 Away! take heed;
 I will abroad.
Call in thy death's-head there; tie up thy fears;
 He that forbears
 To suit and serve his need
 Deserves his load.
But as I raved and grew more fierce and wild

At every word,

Methought I heard one calling, *Child!*

And I replied *My Lord.*

January 25th

This was an impulsive choice- seeing Henry Wooton's name on a list and thinking of the only poem of his I know. In fact, if not his only poem, it's the only one remembered today. It's a charming conceit, but when you know its subject is Elizabeth, daughter of James 1st, you sense sycophancy raising its oily head. Especially as none of the Stuarts was conspicuous for beauty.

Yet this is unfair. Wooton, a diplomat, was apparently deeply sincere in his admiration for this princess. And as I follow her story, I'm led on a marvellous journey, through masques and mazes, singing fountains, tragedy and loss.

Elizabeth first came to prominence as a very small child, when she was the intended target of the Gunpowder plotters. They aimed to kidnap her, bring her up as a Catholic and eventually put her on the throne of a Catholic England. And every schoolboy knew – probably still knows - what happened to that ill-starred lot.

But then, for a few later years, her life was a true fairy tale. Her wedding in 1613 to the young Frederick V, Elector Palatine of the Rhine, was the most glamorous event of its day, far outshining our own royal weddings. There were weeks and weeks of celebrations, masques, fireworks and music.(It's possible that the wedding masque in *The Tempest* was intended for them.) On her wedding day, the bride wore '*a crown of refined golde, made imperiall by the pearles and diamonds thereupon placed, which were so thicke beset that they stood like shining pinnacles upon her amber coloured haire, dependently hanging playted downe over her shoulders to her waste.*' In addition, unusually for a royal match, the young couple were deeply in love, and remained so all their lives.

Then they journeyed sumptuously to Frederick's court in Heidelberg, where they constructed magical gardens, the glory of their day, with speaking statues, musical fountains and fantastic grottoes. All this came to an end however, when Frederick was persuaded to claim the crown of Bohemia – things went suddenly desperately wrong and at the end of just over a year, everything was over for the 'Winter Queen' and her husband. They even lost their own Palatinate lands, and spent the rest of their lives in exile; the statues fell silent, the fountains crumbled, the walks were overgrown.

As a bonus, I Google the song version of this poem. I find it on YouTube sung by the incomparable Emma Kirkby, set to music by Michael East. Delicious.

You Meaner Beauties of the Night   **Sir Henry Wooton**

You meaner beauties of the night,
That poorly satisfy our eyes
More by your number than your light;
You common people of the skies,
What are you when the sun shall rise?

You curious chanters of the wood,
That warble forth Dame Nature's lays,
Thinking your voices understood

By your weak accents; what's your praise
When Philomel her voice shall raise?

You violets that first appear,
By your pure purple mantles known,
Like the proud virgins of the year,
As if the spring were all your own;
What are you when the rose is blown?

So, when my mistress shall be seen
In form and beauty of her mind,
By virtue first, then choice, a queen,
Tell me, if she were not design'd
Th' eclipse and glory of her kind?

January 26th

Impossible to ignore that we're in the midst of one of the worst winters I remember. Snow falls, thaws slightly, then falls again. Some days the roads are gritted and we can make tentative little forays in the car – too icy to walk – to the supermarket car park, where we slither off to do our bit of shopping and scurry home again to hot coffee and wood fires. It's a strange half-existence, where managing the everyday world becomes fraught with difficulties.

And yet, at least on those days when the sun shines, it's stunningly beautiful. A polished turquoise sky, and the light on the snow-covered hill changing throughout the day, dazzling white at first, becoming lilac, pink and soft grey as the shadows pass across.

Here's a snow poem I remember from my schooldays; it sums up the wonder of that first, unexpected glimpse of snow, and the transformation of a familiar landscape.

London Snow   Robert Bridges

When men were all asleep the snow came flying
In large white flakes falling on the city brown,
Stealthily and perpetually settling and loosely lying,
       Hushing the latest traffic of the drowsy town:
Deadening, muffling, stifling its murmurs failing:
Lazily and incessantly floating down and down:
       Silently sifting and veiling road, roof and railing:
Hiding difference, making unevenness even,
Into angles and crevices softly drifting and sailing.
       All night it fell, and when full inches seven
It lay in the depth of its uncompacted lightness,
The clouds blew off from a high and frosty heaven:
       And all woke earlier for the unaccustomed brightness
Of the winter dawning, the strange unheavenly glare:
The eye marvelled – marvelled at the dazzling whiteness;
       The ear hearkened to the stillness of the solemn air:
No sound of wheel rumbling nor of foot falling,
And the busy morning cries came thin and spare.
       Then boys I heard, as they went to school, calling,
They gathered up the crystal manna to freeze
Their tongues with tasting, their hands with snowballing:
       Or rioted in a drift, plunging up to the knees;
Or peering up from under the white-mossed wonder,

'O look at the trees!' they cried 'O look at the trees!'

With lessened load a few carts creak and blunder,
Following along the white deserted way,
A country company long dispersed asunder;

When now already the sun, in pale display
Standing by Paul's high dome, spread forth below
His sparkling beams, and awoke the stir of the day.

For now doors open and war is waged with the snow:
And trains of sombre men, past tale of number,
Tread long brown paths, as toward their toil they go;

But even for them awhile no cares encumber
Their minds diverted, the daily word is unspoken,
The daily thoughts of labour and sorrow slumber
At the sight of the beauty that greets them, for the charm they have
broken.

January 22nd

Wilfred Owen today. Instead of his more famous war poems, I find
this. With its gems and purples and lamps and dusks it's the poem
of a young man courting decadence, but I like the mood and
mystery of it. Owen wasn't a Londoner; what did Shadwell mean to
him? The firm-fleshed shadow with tumultuous eyes walking
through the night sounds like a prostitute, and since Owen was gay,
maybe it's a young man. Gay men must have felt like ghosts in a
London that pretended they didn't exist. But speculation apart, it's
eerily memorable.

Shadwell Stair   Wilfred Owen

I am the ghost of Shadwell Stair.
        Along the wharves by the water-house,
        And through the cavernous slaughter-house,
I am the shadow that walks there.

    Yet I have flesh both firm and cool,
        And eyes tumultuous as the gems
        Of moons and lamps in the full Thames
When dusk sails wavering down the pool.

Shuddering the purple street-arc burns
        Where I watch always; from the banks
        Dolorously the shipping clanks
And after me a strange tide turns.

I walk till the stars of London wane
        And dawn creeps up the Shadwell Stair.
        But when the crowing syrens blare
I with another ghost am lain.

January 29th

We're going to a village funeral this afternoon – Charles, who died last week was 102. He'd been a blacksmith and a fine craftsman, though his great love was religion. When he came to tea, he'd ask permission to say grace, and then , very still and upright, would thank the Lord at great length for just about everything. If you visited, he'd press tracts into your hand. You'd expect a blacksmith to be big and brawny; but Charles was slim and rather elegant, an old fashioned gentleman, who would kiss your hand on meeting. There seemed no reason why he shouldn't have lived for many years more. That last day, he got up as usual, shaved, read his Bible, had his lunch, sat down in a chair. Then he had a coughing fit, and died. A century and two years, all that experience, all those memories, over just like that.

Death, not surprisingly, is the subject of many poems. I feel I'd like to have one from the volume I once saw advertised in a second-hand bookseller's catalogue; a book of memorial poems, 'the wrapper worn and rubbed with small tears.'

But this is a moving poem from the seventeenth century Henry King, written after the death of his beloved wife.

From   The Exequy   Henry King

Sleep on my *Love* in thy cold bed
Never to be disquieted!
My last good night! Thou wilt not wake
Till I thy fate shall overtake:
Till age, or grief, or sickness must
Marry my body to that dust
It so much loves; and fill the room
My heart keeps empty in thy Tomb.
Stay for me there; I will not faile
To meet thee in that hollow Vale.
And think not much of my delay:
I am already on the way,
And follow thee with all the speed
Desire can make, or sorrows breed.
Each minute is a short degree,
And ev'ry houre a step towards thee.
At night when I betake to rest,

Next morn I rise neerer my West
Of life, almost by eight houres saile,
Than when sleep breath'd his drowsie gale.

February

February 7th

I'm staying in London, with only a couple of poetry books on the shelves. One is the *Faber Book of Children's Verse*, edited by Janet Adam Smith, and it started me thinking of the poetry I read at school and those poetry lessons.

I knew just one excellent teacher, in my life, when I was nine or ten. He was unfortunately named Mr Birchmore, but in those days when teachers were seldom kind, he was never anything other than gentle and inspirational. With him, we read *Hans Brinker and the Silver Skates* – I remember nothing of the story but retain an image of the dazzle of ice and the hiss of blades. He told us of the Emerald City where a wonderful wizard waited (and how disappointed I was years later to find out what that wizard was really like) He played us a crackly gramophone record of a little girl, the same age as us!- singing a song in a crystal clear mature voice – looking back I think it might have been the young Julie Andrews. He told us a haunting story of a little princess whose grave had been uncovered in Westminster Abbey. As the coffin lid was lifted, she was, just for a moment, perfectly visible, even the flowers she'd been buried with. Then the air rushed in, and she crumbled into dust. He could draw; when I left his class he made a lovely pencil drawing of kittens for my autograph album, which to my shame I lost a few years later.

But most memorably, he told us how a poet transformed the ordinary, and saw things in a different way from the rest of us, which made me feel that a poet must be a good thing to be. As an example he read us Walter de la Mare's *'Suppose'* and paused on the lines:

> '... *when the gentle star of evening*
> *Came crinkling into the blue.....*

Only a poet, he said, would think of using that word 'crinkling,' to describe the movement of a star in the sky. I've never re-read the poem since that day over sixty years ago, but those two lines stayed with me, as has the idea of poets as people who make magical use of humdrum things.

After Mr Birchmore, it was downhill all the way as far as school poetry was concerned.. Poetry came once a week, regular as clockwork, and we worked through a series of books : *'Poetry Today'*, I think, books one, two , three and four, until the fifth year when we had *A Pageant of Modern Verse* which wasn't particularly modern. Then there was learning by heart. I don't suppose anyone does that now, and yet how nice to have those poems in your head.

Elocution lessons were another way of abusing poetry. I went to classes for years, to no very good purpose. I'd inherited perfectly good RP pronunciation from my parents, and as for standing up and performing, I enjoyed it – and would do it- up to the age when I suddenly didn't and wouldn't. It wasn't a useful skill, and had nothing to do with acting; we learned poems with odd and inappropriate stresses, and over-mannered gestures. My party piece was: *Through the FOREST have I gone, But ATHENIAN found I NONE On whose eyes I might APPROVE This flower's force in STIRRING LOVE. Night and SILENCE! Who is HERE? Weeds of ATHENS he doth wear ...*

Janet Adam Smith's book, although it's aimed at children, contains poems that would have given me the screaming abjabs as a child, and still today make me turn the page quickly. Here's one I'm not going to quote; it involves a cat , and isn't very nice. To console myself, I find a beautiful cat poem, Yeats' *The Cat and the Moon*, one of his early magical ones, seduced by the sing-song of words, and their power. I love the way the cat's eyes echo the phases of the moon and the dancing link between them. Along with Jeoffry and Panguar Ban, Minnaloushe is one of the great poetry-cats.

The Cat and the Moon   W.B. Yeats

The cat went here and there
And the moon spun round like a top,
And the nearest kin of the moon,
The creeping cat, looked up.
Black Minnaloushe stared at the moon,
For, wander and wail as he would,
The pure cold light in the sky
Troubled his animal blood.
Minnaloushe runs in the grass
Lifting his delicate feet.
Do you dance, Minnaloushe, do you dance?
When two close kindred meet,
What better than call a dance?
Maybe the moon may learn,
Tired of that courtly fashion,
A new dance turn.
Minnaloushe creeps through the grass
From moonlit place to place,
The sacred moon overhead

Has taken a new phase.
Does Minnaloushe know that his pupils
Will pass from change to change,
And that from round to crescent,
From crescent to round they range?
Minnaloushe creeps through the grass
Alone, important and wise,
And lifts to the changing moon
His changing eyes.

February 9th

Today's book was The Rattle Bag, edited by Seamus Heaney and Ted Hughes, and given to me, I note with pleasure, by my elder daughter, one Christmas years ago. This came off the shelf at random, but the poem didn't. I leafed through the book, glimpsed this poem, saw what it was about, and turned the page. But it hung in my mind, so I went back and read it properly. Then I decided I couldn't choose it; it was too upsetting.

Then I realised that the poem had got to me, which is what poems are supposed to do, and so I had no right to ignore it. I had tried hard not to chose it, but it had chosen me, and here it is.

Bags of Meat   Thomas Hardy

'Here's a fine bag of meat,'
Says the master-auctioneer,
As the timid, quivering steer,
Starting a couple of feet
At the prod of a drover's stick,
And trotting lightly and quick,

A ticket stuck on his rump
Enters with a bewildered jump

'Where he's lived lately, friends,
I'd live till lifetime ends:
They've a whole life everyday,
Down there in the Vale, have they!
He'd be worth the money to kill
And give away Christmas for goodwill.'

'Now here's a heifer – worth more
Than bid, were she bone-poor;
Yet she's round as a barrel of beer';
'She's a plum,' said the second auctioneer.
'Now this young bull – for thirty pound?
Worth that to manure your ground!'
'Or to stand,' chimed the second one,'
And have his picter done!'

The beast was rapped on the horns and snout
To make him turn about.
'Well, ' cried a buyer , 'another crown –
Since I've dragged here from Taunton Town!'

'That calf, she sucked three cows,
Which is not matched for bouse
In the nurseries of high life
By the first born of a nobleman's wife!'

The stick falls, meaning 'A true tale's told,'
On the buttock of the creature sold,
And the buyer leans over and snips
His mark on one of the animal's hips.
Each beast, when driven in,
Looks round at the ring of bidders there
With a much- amazed reproachful stare,
As at unnatural kin,
For bringing him to a sinister scene
So strange, unhomelike, hungry, mean;
His fate the while suspended between
A butcher , to kill out of hand,
And a farmer, to keep on the land:
One can fancy a tear runs down his face,
When the butcher wins, and he's driven from the place.

February 10th

I stay with *The Rattle Bag* today, and find a poem by which has been called the saddest in the English language. I don't think it's quite that - Ben Jonson's poem (*rest in soft peace, and asked, say here doth lie/ Ben Jonson his best piece of poetry..)* on the death of his first-born, holds that place for me, but it's a heartbreaking read, nonetheless. Chidiock Tichborne, from an ancient family, was a staunch Catholic and involved in the Babington Plot to establish Mary Queen of Scots on the throne. He was arrested, and on his last night alive, wrote this poem, with its haunting rhythms and accumulated antitheses, from the Tower, and enclosed it in a letter sent to his wife Agnes. It's rhetorical, but infused with real passion.

He was in his early thirties. His death was horrible – the hanging, drawing and quartering reserved for traitors; though apparently Queen Elizabeth changed her mind halfway through this gruesome series of executions and ordained that the other traitors be simply hanged.

It's an odd poem for a Catholic to write – you'd expect he'd find reconciliation in the thought of the martyr's crown, which gains you the highest place in heaven. But this poem is without consolation . He's young, he doesn't want to die, but he's going to. That's it: devastating.

My Prime of Youth Chidiock Tichborne

My prime of youth is but a frost of cares;
  My feast of joy is but a dish of pain:
My crop of corn is but a field of tares;
  And all my good is but vain hopes of gain:
The day is past, and yet I saw no sun;
And now I live, and now my life is done.

My tale was heard, and yet it was not told;
  My fruit is fall'n, and yet my leaves are green;
My youth is spent, and yet I am not old;
I saw the world, and yet I was not seen:
My thread is cut, and yet it is not spun;
And now I live, and now my life is done.

I sought my death, and found it in my womb;
  I looked for life, and saw it was a shade;

I trod the earth, and knew it was my tomb;
And now I die, and now I was but made;
My glass is full, and now my glass is run;
And now I live, and now my life is done.

February 11th

Today's poem chooses itself – or rather chose itself, last night, as we drove home on an achingly cold, blindingly clear night. The Radnor hills were powdered with a dusting of snow, and the stars blazed down. The night before, we'd been watching *The Sky At Night* about Mars, which just now is very clear and easy to see in the night sky. We stood there, shivering, but entranced, found the saucepan-edge of the Plough, and moved our eyes sideways, and there it was, huge and dazzling, though vermillion-orange rather than the ruby-red I'd imagined. I wonder if Earth shines blue in the sky of Mars..

The poem running through my head all that night car journey through was Browning's '*My Star.*' This had been a favourite poem when I was a child, and I still look out for Browning's star that 'dartles the red and the blue.' Sometimes I think I see it ; there's a star low in the summer sky, but it flashes emerald and red rather than blue. I never knew what the 'angled spar' was , until a couple of years ago, when we saw it in souvenir shops on a holiday in Derbyshire.

For Browning, who can be irritatingly obscure, this is (nearly) a simple poem. You do wonder, though, why can't he show his friends the star? Why must they settle for Saturn? Never mind. It's mesmeric. I must try to find out which star it is. I need a tame astronomer

My Star   Robert Browning

All that I know
  Of a certain star
Is, it can throw
  (Like the angled spar)
Now a dart of red,
  Now a dart of blue:
Till my friends have said
They would fain see, too,
My star that dartles the red and the blue!
Then it stops like a bird; like a flower hangs furled:
  They must solace themselves with the Saturn above it.
What matter to me if their star is a world?
  Mine has opened its soul to me; therefore I love it.

February 14th

Impossible to ignore Valentine's Day. Today though it's a Sunday and we're off to our little twelfth century church for a service. St Paul is there, too, and the famous Letter to the Corinthians which makes much more sense now that the word 'love' rather than the bewildering 'charity' is used as its theme. Our local retired bishop takes the service today and he tells us of the three Greek words for love, *eros*, erotic love, *philos*, friendship, and *agape*, a kind of noble transcendent love, and it's this last one that is used in the Greek text. We learn too about St Valentine, a Roman centurion, condemned to death by a wicked emperor, because he encouraged soldiers to marry, against the law at the time. While he was in prison, he miraculously cured his jailer's daughter of her blindness. Some sources say that before he went to his execution, he sent her a letter signed 'From Your Valentine.' Then the Bishop charms and surprises us by finishing off with a slightly risqué love poem. All quite heady for a Sunday morning

There are so many love poems – Shakespeare's sonnets, Elizabeth Barrett Browning counting the ways, Christina Rossetti's heart like a singing bird. And of course the Song Of Solomon from the King James Bible, surely the most sexy poem in English, *and* in the Bible too. Also Emily Dickinson's beautiful 'Love, Thou art High.' But for sheer yearning and longing, it's hard to beat these four haunting lines from an anonymous medieval poet - it sounds like a woman's voice to me:

Western Wind   Anon
Western wind, when wilt thou blow,
The small rain down can rain?
Christ, if my love were in my arms
And I in my bed again!

February 16th

February 16th
Sitting in the car, we listen to a rather lugubrious, but dramatic setting by a modern composer of a poem. I recognise the poem, which is easy, and Richard recognises the composer, which is impressive. He's John Adams who wrote *Nixon in China* The setting

suits the poem, though, it just isn't very cheery on a cold grey morning and a crisp layer of ice like tissue paper on the car.

I still remember the shock of excitement on first reading Donne's love poems as a teenager. Did poets really write like this? And four hundred years ago! Then it was disappointing to know that he'd repudiated his love poems at the end of his life; though fortunately for us he hadn't destroyed them. The Donne that emerges from the pages of the recent excellent biography by John Stubbs is a self-dramatising, histrionic figure, not averse to a little social climbing. Of course as a young widower with young children to provide for, he had to move onwards and upwards as best he could. And his sermonising must have been mesmeric – fancy actually standing in Paul's Churchyard, and actually hearing those words about the tolling bell.

To modern eyes this poem takes an exaggerated and unnecessarily dark view of his salvation. But it's impossible for us to inhabit a seventeenth century mind, and know that real sense of sin and eternity and a wrathful God waiting to pounce. And Death ever to hand, in the form of plagues, fits and fevers. Beauty and despair and corruption.... For a few moments as we read this sonnet, we can almost become seventeenth century souls ourselves.

I print it in the original spelling because somehow the sigh of that long drawn out 'mee' , and its melancholy solipsism seems essential to the spirit of this poem.

Holy Sonnet XIV   John Donne

Battter my heart, three-person'd God, for you

As yet but knocke, breathe, shine, and seeke to mend;

That I may rise and stand, o'erthrow mee, and bend

Your force to breake, blowe, burn, and make mee new.

I, like an usurpt towne to'another due,

Labor to'admit you, but Oh, to no end;

Reason your viceroy in mee, me should defend,

But is captiv'd, and proves weake or untrue.

Yet dearly I love you, and would be lov'd faine,

But am betroth'd unto your enemie;

Divorce mee, untie or breake that knot againe,

Take mee to you, imprison mee, for I,

Except you'enthrall mee, never shall be free,

Nor ever chast, except you ravish mee

February 22nd

I'm going to be sitting in a train today, and this is the poem that always runs through my head as we hurtle through the countryside. Robert Louis Stevenson's children's poems capture that childhood sense of the new and extraordinary, probably because he was a sick child who spent long days in bed, remembering things

The journey I'm going on today – Cardiff to Paddington – is the same journey I used to make in reverse for childhood holidays in South Wales. I remember the big panting shiny trains, lungfuls of sulphur smoke, the rain of grit, the dirty glass roof, tea urns and currant buns under glass domes, machines that stamped out your name on a strip of metal letters. Being a *gurl* and not a train spotter,

I didn't find any of this especially romantic. But train journeys were romantic, wondering who people were and where they were going; the middle aged lady with her thick stockings and stiff smile, a bunch of chrysanths in her wicker basket, the children kicking each other under the table, the young woman surreptitiously wiping away a tear. Mobile phones have taken away much of that romance – alas, these days you know far too much about every passenger.

Much of what Stevenson saw we see today, although the new high speed trains make the wrong noise for the rhythm of the poem. I read somewhere that when trains were new, cattle did rush away from them in fright – now they graze peacefully as we thunder past ; they're used to us. But stations still rush by as you try in vain to read the names, children clamber, daisies sparkle in the meadows. Houses, factories, supermarkets, motorways, churches, nestling farms, gleaming streams. Each a glimpse and gone forever!

From a Railway Carriage   Robert Louis Stevenson

Faster than fairies, faster than witches,
Bridges and houses, hedges and ditches;
And charging along like troops in a battle
All through the meadows the horses and cattle:
All of the sights of the hill and the plain
Fly as thick as driving rain:
And ever again, in the wink of an eye,
Painted stations whistle by.
Here is a child who clambers and scrambles,
All by himself and gathering brambles;
Here is a tramp who stands and gazes;

And here is the green for stringing the daisies!
Here is a cart runaway in the road
Lumping along with man and load;
And here is a mill, and there is a river,
Each a glimpse and gone forever!

February 27th

I asked Richard to find me a poem the other day, and he gave me this, by Hopkins. But today, he's in hospital, so it will be an anxious weekend .

Since *'Hurrahing in Harvest'* I've been re-reading the biography of Hopkins by Robert Bernard Martin. Both this poem, and *Hurrahing in Harvest* were written in the wonderfully productive years 1876-7 when Hopkins was studying at St Beuno's college near St Asaph's. Although Hopkins wasn't at all Welsh, he said he felt as though he was, and even learned Welsh – not easy, as I can testify. For him, Wales was the 'mother of Muses.' The patterns of Welsh poetry can be seen in his own. *When kingfishers catch fire, dragonflies draw flame* is an attempt at *cynghanedd* ('harmony') in which the consonants of the first half of the line are repeated in the same order in the second ; hard to do in Welsh and almost impossible in English.

In St Beuno's, Hopkins was in his eighth year as a Jesuit novice. As a child, he'd been ardent, affectionate and happy. But religion had always threaded itself through his life, and when he became an undergraduate, he fell into the company of other young men who were enthusiastically High Anglican, in those years when religion demanded excessive and neurotic examination of conscience. The fact that his romantic feelings were directed towards other young men meant that sexual love was for him inexorably associated with Sin. But his religious feelings were real enough, and his move towards the Catholic church and the Jesuits seems to have been a logical progression of his thoughts rather than an escape into necessary celibacy. As Martin says; 'Once begun, a course of moral action, particularly a difficult one, had to run its full length before he could let it go in peace.'

In this poem he might be recalling a visit of 1864, when he walked the countryside near Bala with two undergraduate friends. He describes in a letter how *'a river ran across the road and cut me off entirely. I took refuge in a shepherd's hut and slept among the Corinthians. They, I mean the shepherd and family, gorged me with eggs and bacon and oaten cake and curds and whey.'* He slept rough under a harsh blanket. You sense the rather smug excitement of the young middle-class boy who's managed to encounter a glimpse of peasant life, and you wonder if he then appreciated the sacrifice they probably made to feed their young visitors.

It's a quieter, more contemplative poem than others of this period; no exuberant language, no scrambled syntax, no complex rhythms; a meditation on kindness, human and divine, and his own sense of unworthiness of both. A modern reader regrets that nineteenth century stress on sinfulness, but it's a calm poem, to allay anxieties

In the Valley of the Elwy   Gerard Manley Hopkins

I remember a house where all were good
> To me, God knows, deserving no such thing:
> Comforting smell breathed at very entering,

Fetched fresh, as I suppose, off some sweet wood.
That cordial air made those kind people a hood
    All over as a bevy of eggs the mothering wing
    Will, or mild nights the new morsels of spring:
Why, it seemed of course; seemed of right it should.

Lovely the woods, waters, meadows, combes, vales,
All the air things wear that build this world of Wales;
    Only the inmate does not correspond:

God, lover of souls, swaying considerate scales,
Complete thy creature dear O where it fails
Being mighty a master; being a father and fond.

March

March 2nd

We wake up to a white morning – the hillside, the bare trees, the fields all silvery white. But this is frost, not snow, and already a gash of sunshine is staining the summit of the bracken-covered hill a glowing vermilion. I have hopes that the sun will come out today, especially as Richard comes home from hospital.

But I miss colour. I long for daffodils, those wonderful swathes of yellow, even the big stiff modern daffodils that purists hate. After the winter we need their brightness – though in July their colour would seem garish.

The egg-yolk yellow crocuses are out, though, and their bright patches pleased me yesterday as we drove back through Worcestershire. But as I start to clear away the winter's debris in the garden , words keep running through my head : *I still am sore in doubt concerning Spring….* Round and round, as I start to clear away the winter's debris, blackened rosemary, dry fennel stalks light as air, soggy monbretia leaves, mummified cat poo…. *Sore in doubt…sore in doubt.* Though I think Spring might at last be on its way – the rose stems already have thick green buds and the crocuses are pools of gold.

Its not until I look it up that I remember it's Christina Rossetti – she and I lived together for about four years in respectful but slightly chill companionship when I was writing a book about her, so I really should have remembered it.

Spring   Christina Rossetti

I wonder if the sap is stirring yet,
If wintry birds are dreaming of a mate,
If frozen snowdrops feel as yet the sun
And crocus fires are kindling one by one:
  Sing, robin, sing;
I still am sore in doubt concerning Spring.

I wonder if the springtide of this year
Will bring another Spring both lost and dear;
If heart and spirit will find out their Spring,
Or if the world alone will bud and sing:
  Sing, hope, to me;
Sweet notes, my hope, soft notes for memory.

The sap will surely quicken soon or late,
The tardiest bird will twitter to a mate;
So Spring must dawn again with warmth and bloom,
Or in this world, or in the world to come:
  Sing, voice of Spring,
Till I too blossom and rejoice and sing.

March 3rd

No particular reason to have this poem today, except that it's one I
love, and it has to appear somewhere in my poetry year

Overheard on a Saltmarsh   Harold Monro

Nymph, nymph, what are your beads?

Green glass, goblin. Why do you stare at them?

Give them me.

No.

Give them me. Give them me.

No.

Then I will howl all night in the reeds,

Lie in the mud and howl for them.

Goblin, why do you love them so?

They are better than stars or water,

Better than voices of winds that sing,

Better than any man's fair daughter,

Your green glass beads on a silver ring.

Hush, I stole them out of the moon.

Give me your beads, I want them.

No.

I will howl in the deep lagoon

For your green glass beads, I love them so.

Give them me. Give them.

No.

March 4th

Today is World Book Day. Everywhere children's writers are polishing up their notes and their shoes, checking powerpoints, practising their reading-aloud-skills, choosing which jewellery, or tie, to wear (friendly without looking too mad or too smart or too writer-y) thinking up new ways of fending off the inevitable questions; *where do you get your ideas from? Do you earn lots of money? Do you sit down and write every day?* And then, always, there's a child who comes out with some wonderful, heart stopping comment or question and suddenly it all makes sense.

Off to Clifford, birthplace of Fair Rosamund, to talk to children there. And here's Chaucer's prayer, at the end of one of his long poems, which must also be the prayer of every writer since; wherever you're read, little book, please God, may you be understood!

From **Troilus and Criseyde** **Geoffrey Chaucer**

Go, litel book, go litel myn tragedie,
    Ther god thy maker yet, er that he dye,
So sende might to make in som comedie!
    But litel book, no making thou nenvye,
But subgit be to alle poesye;
    And kis the steppes, wher-as thou seest pace
Virgile, Ovyde, Omer, Lucan, and Stace.

And for ther is so greet diversitee
    In English and in wryting of our tonge,
So preye I god that noon miswryte thee,
    Ne thee mismetre for defaute of tonge.
And red wher-so thou be, or elles songe,
    That thou be understonde I god beseche!

March 5th

A book of poetry arrived in the post yesterday, a present from our friends Tony and Sarah Thomas. Tony has also been in hospital recently, and he hoped the book would cheer up Richard's recuperation as it had cheered up his own. By the rules of serendipity that I've set myself, this must be the book from which I chose today's poem. It is Lord Wavell's *Other Men's Flowers*, published in 1944, one of the most popular anthologies of the last century. Wavell was a Field Marshall, who loved poetry, and he assembled this collection of his personal favourites. The collection expanded; friends and family advised. All of the poems he'd once known by heart – an impressive feat; how many even avid poetry readers could match that today? I wish I had all the poems of my choice by heart, or even most of them. Poetry should be declaimed, he said; it was a necessary part of its function.

Wavell's taste was solidly conservative and old-fashioned. Indeed this book could largely have been assembled thirty years earlier. He thought much of Eliot was 'deliberately ugly as well as cryptic.' No Eliot, then, but much Browning, Kipling, Macauley, Chesterton, Masefield. It's a little window into middle-class English taste of a certain period.

I read this poem at school, though I'd forgotten it until now. I think I'd learned it by heart, too, though unlike with Lord Wavell, it hasn't stuck. But it's gently familiar to me as I read it now; those brown slaves and Syrian oranges. There are lovely colours in this poem, the soft blue-greens and golds. Though I remember I didn't like the harshness of black Cyprus and the ring of fire – it seemed too much like a calendar photograph to me then. And now, I'm not too sure about the metaphor in the last lines – the poem is rich enough without that rather awkward image.

The Old Ships   James Elroy Flecker

I have seen old ships sail like swans asleep
Beyond the village which men still call Tyre,
With leaden age o'ercargoed, dipping deep
For Famagusta and the hidden sun
That rings black Cyprus with a lake of fire;
And all those ships were certainly so old
Who knows how oft with squat and noisy gun,
Questing brown slaves or Syrian oranges,
The pirate Genoese
Hell-raked them till they rolled
Blood, water, fruit and corpses up the hold.
But now through friendly seas they softly run,
Painted the mid-sea blue or shore-sea green,
Still patterned with the vine and grapes in gold.
But I have seen,
Pointing her shapely shadows from the dawn
And image tumbled on a rose-swept bay,
A drowsy ship of some yet older day;
Thought I –who knows- who knows- but in that same
(Fished up beyond Aeaea , patched up new
-Stern painted brighter blue-)
That talkative, bald-headed seaman came
(Twelve patient comrades sweating at the oar)

From Troy's doom-crimson shore,
And with great lies about his wooden horse
Set the crew laughing and forgot his course.
It was so old a ship – who knows –who knows?
-And yet so beautiful, I watched in vain
To see the mast burst open with a rose,
And the whole deck put on its leaves again.

March 12th

We're hoping to go to Suffolk tomorrow, probably my favourite English county. I love the huge skies, the way land and sea leach into each other, the reed-beds, the upturned boats, the platinum sheen of water, the water-fowl. It feels Anglo-Saxon , though of course it has older and older histories (Don't tell me that the village of Iken doesn't get its name from the Iceni) The site of Sutton Hoo, though it's been tidied up and National Trustified, is still one of the most evocative of walks, as you picture the great boat being hauled up the shallow slope from the river Debden. Years ago, walking there I bent down and picked up a random piece of flint and made a joke about it being an arrow head. Actually it wasn't, but it was a beautifully-made little scraper, curved to fit neatly into the palm of a small hand, a woman's hand, I think. I imagine my bronze-age housewife patiently scraping away at a deer-hide before her hearth-fire, hundreds of years before the Saxons arrived, or Boudicca, or the Romans. You find these things in the strangest places – the other day my granddaughter solemnly handed me a worked flint scraper from the sandpit in Highbury Fields where she was playing with her bucket and spade.

Of course, all lands are ancient lands in a way, but you don't always sense that –it's hard to feel the pulse of history as you drive round the North Circular or the Birmingham motorways.

I think of this owl poem when I think of Suffolk, and I was wondering where I'd find it. Last night came two nice little bits of synchronicity. We don't often see owls, though we hear them, but yesterday when I went to put the chickens to bed at six-thirty, I felt a disturbance of the air in the aspen trees, and there was that great black silhouette and the unmistakable heavy flapping flight. Later, I saw it perched on a high wire with its big round head, watching me, imperturbably from a safe distance.

And that evening I opened my new anthology at random and there it was; my owl poem.

Sweet Suffolk Owl   **Anon**
Sweet Suffolk owl, so trimly dight
With feathers like a lady bright,
Thou sing'st alone, sitting by night
      Te whit, te whoo! Te whit, te whoo!

Thy note that forth so freely rolls
With shrill command the mouse controls
And sings a dirge for dying souls,
      Te whit, te whoo! Te whit, te whoo!

March 16th
Is there a drearier road in Britain than the A14; unspooling from the toxic motorways of Birmingham, then taking off for mile after

flat and featureless mile, never a town or a village or a landmark, litter-strewn, drunken lines of traffic cones, and dirty plastic bags snagged in the trees like little grey lost souls?

Once we took the wrong turning and finding ourselves in the countryside around Little Gidding, scored off another in our Four Quartets collection. (the other two were the golden and cosy East Coker and the grey and windy Dry Salvages), but had no time to explore and so soon we were back on the road and Little Chefs and high-sided swaying lorries.

Suffolk rewarded us with one of its beautiful days, a polished blue sky and silvery reflections. We walked, as I'd hoped around Sutton Hoo. Hares jumped out of the grass before us and bounded away. There were gaunt and gnarled pine trees on the horizon and huge trees fallen on the ground. Light flooded us, reflected from sea and river.

Maldon is a long way from Suffolk, but I was reminded of these magnificent lines, spoken by the aged warrior Byrhtwold, urging his fellow warriors to bravery even though the day is going badly, one of the finest poetic examples of finding triumph in defeat.

From   The Battle of Maldon   Anon

Byrhtwold mapelode, bord hafenode-
Se waes eald geneat —aesc acwehte
He ful baldlice beornas laerde:
Hige sceal þe heardra, heortre þe cenre
Mod sceal þe mare þe ure maegen lytiað.
Her lið ure ealdor eall forhewen,
God on greote. A maeg gnornian

Se ðe nu fram þis wigplegan wendan þenceð.
Ic eom frod feorest; fram ic ne wille
Ac ic me be healfe minum hlaforde
Be swa leofan men licgan þence.

Byrhtwold spoke; held high his shield
Shaking his ash-spear, loyal old man.
Boldly he pleaded, urged on his warriors;

'Minds shall be mightier, hearts shall be keener,
Courage shall be greater, as our strength grows less.
Here lies our leader, hacked all to pieces,
Great on the ground. Let him mourn ever
Who from this battleplay thinketh to flee.
I am an old man, but I will not turn,
And I mean now to lie by the side of my lord,
Near so many loved ones…

March 17th

We stayed in Suffolk with dear friends Barbara and Jemma. Barbara is a great fan of Walt Whitman, and every so often goes off alone to spend the day reading Walt Whitman under a quiet tree somewhere with a bottle of champagne.

I have mixed feelings about the great Walt. Literature certainly needed him in the 19th century to break the confines of Tennysonianism and set poetry free. It must have been exhilarating and slightly scary to be one of his first readers. *Do I contradict myself? Very well, I contradict myself. I am large, I contain multitudes….* But he doesn't half go on. Some of those long rants remind me of Christopher Smart, wonderful but insane, and Blake, who also wasn't entirely sane a lot of the time.

Anyway, here are two bits of Walt Whitman. The first is Barbara's choice, and reflects her love of animals and her ability to find joy in the miniature perfections of nature: the second is a poem that I found, and liked for being gentle, unpretentious and perceptive.

From   Song of Myself   Walt Whitman

I believe a leaf of grass is no less than the journey work of the stars,
And the pismire is equally perfect, and a grain of sand, and the egg of the wren,
And the tree-toad is a chef –d'oeuvre for the highest,
And the running blackberry would adorn the parlours of heaven,
And the narrowest hinge in my hand puts to scorn all machinery,
And the cow crunching with depress'd head surpasses any statue,
And a mouse is miracle enough to stagger sextillions of infidels.

(pismire – ant)

Beginners   Walt Whitman

How they are provided for upon the earth (appearing at intervals;)

How dear and dreadful they are to the earth;

How they inure to themselves as much as to any – what a paradox appears their age;

How people respond to them, yet know them not;

How there is something relentless in their fate, at all times;

How at all times mischoose the objects of their adulation and reward,

And how the same inexorable price must still be paid for the same great purchase.

March 22nd

The Welsh border where we live is full of mysteries. Driving in through the flatlands of the Wye valley in Herefordshire, you see that dark scribble of hills on the horizon, and you know that behind their barrier, everything's different, place names, architecture, landscape. Wales is suddenly there.

But it's not quite Wales, either. It's border Wales, and the accent isn't quite Welsh. Village names are odd and don't break down neatly in either language: Clyro, Cregrina, Rhulen. The hills are deceptively gentle, but can turn suddenly harsh if the mist or rain comes down. Valleys are small, but deeply scoured. The greenness of everything in spring is intense, tiny waterfalls rush down vertical rockfaces. Red kites wheel and turn in the sky.

Prehistoric men and women raised cromlechs and barrows here. Not far from us is the site of one of the greatest wooden enclosures in Britain. The Romans tramped through our valleys, built camps but could never penetrate any further. The Normans studded the border with castles, manned them with robber barons, but didn't get any further either, not till much later. There are prim chapels, as in the rest of Wales, but it's the churches, tiny, whitewashed, named for mysterious, and otherwise unknown saints, which stir the heart.

And the border wavers and wanders over these lands. Sometimes it's obvious as the red dragon welcomes you. Sometimes it's not; you weave in and out of the two countries, never quite sure where you are. Slip behind a rock, and you might well stumble into a cave of sleeping warriors…

It's not surprising that this haunted and fluid landscape has produced so many poets. Three of the greatest metaphysicals are border men – four, if you count, as he did , John Donne's family as being Welsh. But George Herbert, Henry Vaughan and – to some extent -Thomas Traherne, all grew up knowing these soft green hills and rushing streams. Herbert's rhyme in 'The Collar' - *all blasted, all wasted* -works better in a Welsh accent .

More recently, R.S.Thomas darkly haunted the hills near Newtown, though his relationship with the locals could be equivocal. One of the saddest moments in the recent biography of him by Byron Rogers, *The Man Who Went Into The West,* describes how his son Gwidion was torn away from the hills and farms that he loved, to be sent to posh school in England- because the local school wasn't seen as good enough. Gwydion was eight, and devastated. The night before he left, he went round all the local farms and chalked 'Remember me,' on doorsteps.

George Herbert was born in Montgomery castle, in what is now a pretty, black-and-white town. He was well connected- his mother was the Magdalen Herbert to whom Donne wrote so many poems;

his brother , also a poet, was Lord Herbert of Cherbury. As a young boy, his mother took him to Oxford for the sake of his education. George was a precocious scholar, and at the age of eighteen had already graduated from Trinity College, Cambridge. He might have had a dazzling career at court, but instead, took Holy Orders, ending up eventually as parish priest in Bemerton, Wiltshire. Isaac Walton describes his marriage to Jane Danvers thus: 'This Mr Danvers, having known him long, and familiarly, did so much affect him that he often and publickly declar'd a desire that Mr Herbert would marry any of his Nine Daughters, but rather his Daughter Jane, because Jane was his beloved Daughter: and he had often said the same to Mr Herbert himself; and that if he could like her for a wife, and she him for a Husband, Jane should have a double blessing; and Mr Danvers had so often said the like to Jane, and so much commended Mr Herbert to her, that Jane became so much a Platonick, as to fall in love with Mr Herbert unseen….'

Presumably, Herbert did 'like her for a wife' for they married; but did not have a long life together – Herbert was only forty when he died. The simplicity and goodness that is present in his poetry seems to have been inherent in the man, too. He was humble and devout, known to his parishioners as 'holy Mr Herbert.' So many of his poems would make a perfect choice for the day; here is one of them.

The Pulley   George Herbert

    When God at first made man,
Having a glasse of blessings standing by;
Let us (said he) poure on him all we can:
Let the world's riches, which dispersed lie,
    Contract into a span

    So strength first made a way;
Then beauty flow'd, then wisdome, honour, pleasure:
When almost all was out, God made a stay,
Perceiving that alone of all his treasure
    Rest in the bottome lay.

    For if I should (said he)
Bestow this jewell also on my creature,
He would adore my gifts in stead of me,
And rest in Nature, not the God of Nature:
    So both should losers be.

    Yet let him keep the rest,
But keep them with repining restlessnesse:
Let him be rich and wearie, that at least,
If goodness leade him not, yet wearinesse
    May tosse him to my breast.

March 23rd

Henry Vaughan- the Silurist - seems to have been altogether a more complex figure than Herbert. Born in Breconshire, his family were probably related to the Vaughans of Tretower. Vaughan trained as a lawyer, but later practised medicine. His twin brother was an alchemist and a hermetic philosopher- and some of those ideas find their way into Henry's verse. He married twice and lived to a good age. In the Civil war, he seems to have favoured the Royalist side, but had little trust in politics generally (wise man!) His conversion to active religion seems partly to have been inspired by Herbert, as his poetry certainly is. His latter days were soured by unpleasant inter-family litigations, in which he seems to have behaved meanly and nastily – another poet whose life is less beautiful than his poetry.

He lived most of his life in the Brecon hills, which he loved, and is buried in Llansaintffraed church.

They Are All Gone Into The World Of Light   Henry Vaughan
They are all gone into the world of light !
     And I alone sit ling'ring here ;
Their very memory is fair and bright,
     And my sad thoughts doth clear.

It glows and glitters in my cloudy breast,
     Like stars upon some gloomy grove,
Or those faint beams in which this hill is dress'd,
     After the sun's remove.

I see them walking in an air of glory,
     Whose light doth trample on my days :
My days, which are at best but dull and hoary,
     Mere glimmering and decays.

O holy Hope ! and high Humility,
    High as the heavens above !
These are your walks, and you have show'd them me,
    To kindle my cold love.

Dear, beauteous Death ! the jewel of the just,
    Shining nowhere, but in the dark ;
What mysteries do lie beyond thy dust,
    Could man outlook that mark !

He that hath found some fledg'd bird's nest, may know
    At first sight, if the bird be flown ;
But what fair well or grove he sings in now,
    That is to him unknown.

And yet, as angels in some brighter dreams
    Call to the soul when man doth sleep,
So some strange thoughts transcend our wonted themes,
    And into glory peep.

If a star were confin'd into a tomb,
    Her captive flames must needs burn there ;
But when the hand that lock'd her up, gives room,
    She'll shine through all the sphere.

O Father of eternal life, and all
    Created glories under Thee !
Resume Thy spirit from this world of thrall
    Into true liberty.

Either disperse these mists, which blot and fill

My perspective still as they pass :

Or else remove me hence unto that hill

Where I shall need no glass.

March 24th

Thomas Traherne was actually born and bred in Hereford, but since Hereford is almost a Welsh city anyway, and the Herefordshire accent and the Radnorshire accent very similar, he counts as almost-a-Welshman. For some years he was the Rector of Credenhill, near Hereford, a church perched on a daffodil-strewn hill by what is now a busy road. He ended his days as a minister in Teddington. Like Herbert, he was barely forty when he died. He seems to have been a genuinely humble and simple man. On his death-bed, he was asked if he wanted his will made in writing. He replied that 'he had not so much but he could dispose of it by word of mouth.' He gave his best hat to his brother Philip and five shillings to Mary the laundry maid.

At his death, his manuscripts were distributed among his friends, and stored for years on dusty shelves, their location unknown. Then some were found on a roadside bookstall, others rescued literally from a blazing bonfire. I found my copy conventionally enough in a Hay bookshop; but was pleased to see, from the inscription on the title page, that it was a given as a gift from George Yeats, W.B. Yeats' wife , who wrote an inscription in it to a friend in 1919.

Traherne had an intense, Wordsworthian love of Nature and a great joy in recalling the early days of his childhood.

> *How like an angel came I down!*
> *How bright are all things here…*

In his prose *Meditations*, he says 'Natural things are glorious and to know them glorious….The riches of Nature are our souls and bodies, with all their faculties, senses and endowments..' It's as though he internalises the beauties of nature and feels them as part of his being. Being a seventeenth century man, sin and corruption get a mention in his poems, but never spoil his sense of enjoyment and pleasure in the world. I love this poem, in which he describes the world as a place so beautiful even angels are impelled to visit.

The Enquiry   Thomas Traherne

Men may delighted be with springs
While trees and herbs their senses please,
And taste even living nectar in the seas:
May think their members things
Of earthly worth at least, if not divine,
And sing because the earth for them doth shine.

II

But can the Angels take delight,
To see such faces here beneath?
Or can perfumes indeed from dung-hills breathe?
Or is the world a sight
Worthy of them? Then may we mortals be
Surrounded with eternal Clarity.

III

Even holy angels may come down
To walk on Earth and see delights,

That feed and please, even here, their appetites.

    Our joys may make a crown

For them. And in His Tabernacle men may be

Like palms we mingled with the Cherubs see.

IV

    Men's senses are indeed the gems,

    Their praises the most sweet perfumes,

Their eyes the thrones, their hearts the Heavenly rooms,

    Their souls the diadems,

Their tongues the organs which they love to hear,

Their cheeks and faces like to theirs appear.

V

    The wonders which our God hath done,

    The glories of His attributes,

Like dangling apples, or like golden fruits,

    Angelic joys become.

His wisdom shines on Earth; His love doth flow,

Like myrrh or incense, even here below.

VI

    And shall not we such joys possess,

    Which God for men did chiefly make?

The Angels have them only for our sake!

    And yet they all confess

His glory here on Earth to be divine,

And that His Godhead in His works doth shine.

March 26th

We're off to the sea again tomorrow; the Welsh sea this time, Cardigan Bay where the drowned land Cantref Gwaelod used to lie; and that started me thinking about all the drowned-land legends that proliferate around our coast, Lyonnesse and the Breton Ker-ys. The legend of underwater bells finds its way into so many Welsh songs and poems.

One version of the story tells of the king Gwyddno Garanhir, who ruled over a fine land, with sixteen cities, protected from the sea by a series of ditches. One night the king's steward Seythenin got drunk and forgot to close the sluices, causing the whole land to be inundated. Another version blames the king's daughter, the Maiden of the well, Meredid.

Yet you can still see the ancient trees, blackened and twisted, but weirdly intact, that once grew as forests, stranded on the shimmering low tide sands of Borth beach. Many of the inundations happened at the end of the ice-age; the so called 'red lady' of Paviland was buried in caves that once looked over a flat land plain, instead of the sea which now laps at the rocks. Was that too long ago to have found its way into folk-tales?

I like this poem by Flecker, though his associations are a bit muddled – the Nemedians belong to Irish mythology, not Welsh – they're the people believed to have come from Scythia to colonise Ireland, and whose descendants were the Tuatha de Danaan. But modern historians see the essential influences on the coast of Wales as Mediterranean and maritime – Spanish and Phoenician, - rather than coming overland from mainland Europe. Maybe those little dark Welshmen who look so North African or Spanish really were descendants of those ancient sailors.

Drowned lands and underwater bells and lost cities. And not so ancient either: Dunwich, in the sandy and piny edge of Suffolk crumbles away even as you look.

The Welsh Sea   James Elroy Flecker

Far out across Carnarvon bay,
    Beneath the evening waves,
The ancient dead begin their day
    And stream among the graves.

Listen, for they of ghostly speech,
    Who died when Christ was born,
May dance upon the golden beach
    That once was golden corn.

And you may learn of Dyfed's reign,
    And dream Nemedian tales
Of Kings who sailed in ships from Spain
    And lent their swords to Wales.

Listen, for like a golden snake
    The Ocean twists and stirs,
And whispers how the dead men wake
    And call across the years.

March 28th Palm Sunday

We had no intention of going to church today. A pleasant morning – spring sun and fresh sea-salted air – took us to look at the lonely, austere mansion of Nanteos, near Aberystwyth, home for many years of the Holy Grail, so it's said. Unfortunately the Grail, a small wooden dish, has been eaten away – literally – over the years, by people wishing to be cured by its magic. Now its chewed remains are hidden away somewhere unknown.

So our Grail Quest having inevitably failed, we walked instead in the Aeron valley, studded with white wood anemones and tiny lemon-yellow wild daffodils. Later on an impulse, we set off to find the church of St Sulian, where there's a Celtic stone kept in the church. After getting lost several times, we found the village, with its ancient, pre-Christian circular churchyard, and little Victorian church.

Christians talk of 'thin places', where the membrane between heaven and earth feels especially fine-stretched; the church of Pennant Melangell near Bala is one, with its legend of the saint with her maidens, who sheltered a hare beneath her skirts, to save it from the hunters, and won the respect of a prince who gave her the land to build a chapel. Near us, there's the tiny church of St David's, Rhulen, hardly bigger than a garage, with its steeply sloping west wall (sloping less, alas since it had to be rebuilt,) and its sanctuary ring on the door. And also Patrishow, with its dance-of-death murals, its beautiful carved screen, and nearby its Holy Well, supposed to have produced miracles even recently. And now, also, I thought, St Sulien.

When we arrived, we turned the door handle and heard a service in progress. So we crept away and would have been disappointed; but then a woman came out, and invited us in for the end of the service. We sang a Welsh hymn, prayed an English prayer, and were given a palm cross. The vicar wasn't sure where the Celtic stone was, but the parishioners knew, and one of them showed us; tucked away behind the font and a pile of flower- arranging wire, oasis foam and plastic bags; a clear, intricate mazy carving, beautifully preserved. Then we were shown another ancient stone set into the church wall; you could just make out a cross and the word 'IACET', a sacred space that's been sacred for many centuries and in many ways.

But it was the warmth of that Welsh welcome given to nosy strangers that will stay with us; and made me think of Herbert's poem – and of the earlier one of Hopkins.

Love   George Herbert

Love bade me welcome; yet my soul drew back,
    Guiltie of dust and sinne,-
But quick-ey'd Love, observing me grow slack
    From my first entrance in,
Drew nearer to me, sweetly questioning,
    If I lack'd any thing.

A guest, I answer'd, worthy to he here:
    Love said, you shall be he.
I the unkinde, ungratefull? Ah my deare,
    I cannot look on thee.

Love took my hand, and smiling did reply,
    Who made the eyes, but I?

Truth Lord, but I have marr'd them: let my shame
    Go where it doth deserve.
And know you not, sayes Love, who bore the blame?
    My dear, then I will serve.
You must sit down, sayes Love, and taste my meat:
    So I did sit and eat.

April

April 1ˢᵗ Maunday Thursday

The name comes from the Latin word Mandatum – a commandment, via old French *mandé*. The commandment is to be found in St John's Gospel: *if I then, your Lord and Master, have washed your feet, ye ought also to wash one another's feet.*

The charity children in Blake's poem, going two by two, into St Paul's Cathedral, are presumably going for a foot-washing ceremony, wearing their orphan livery. They are innocent, radiant, beautiful. They are flowers of London Town in a Garden of Eden. Their guardians, aged men, are wise.

But this is Blake, and the poem is a *Song of Innocence*. It has a dark twin, in *Songs of Experience*. Here the poem of the same title begins:

> *Is this a holy thing to see*
> *In a rich and fruitful land,*
> *Babes reduc'd to misery*
> *Fed with cold and usurous hand?*

Their 'garden' is 'fill'd with thorns' and endures 'eternal winter' The second poem is probably more true to the lives of charity children, in spite of the kindness of a few figures like the genial Captain Coram. Blake's righteous anger is spilled to powerful effect into the dark corners of urban life.

Holy Thursday   William Blake

'Twas on a Holy Thursday, their innocent faces clean,
The children walking two and two, in red and blue and green,
Grey-headed beadles walk'd before, with wands as white as snow
Till into the high dome of Paul's they like Thames' waters flow.

O what a multitude they seem'd, these flowers of London town!
Seated in companies they sit with radiance all their own.
The hum of multitudes was there, but multitudes of lambs,
Thousands of little boys and girls raising their innocent hands.

Now like a mighty wind they raise to Heaven the voice of song,
Or like harmonious thunderings the seats of Heaven among.
Beneath them sit the aged men, wise guardians of the poor;
Then cherish pity, lest you drive an angel from your door.

April 2nd Good Friday

Apart from a few sonnets, Elizabeth Barratt Browning's poetry isn't much read today. But there's a clear, bright intellect there, which makes you wonder if she wouldn't have been happier a as novelist, able to expound her ideas in greater depth. *Aurora Leigh* is a riveting read, at least for the first few books, after which she falls into slack and sentimental characterisation and melodrama.

For Elizabeth Barratt Browning - after her years of ill-health, her late marriage, her opium addiction, the miscarriages - the birth of her son, the beloved and cosseted Pen, must have seemed like a miracle. Poor Pen, he wasn't the Messiah, just a very naughty boy. After his mother's death his father cut off all his long curls, took him back to London, and subjected him to an intense and solemn upbringing. Pen grew into an amiable, affectionate, slightly bumbling fellow, with a mild artistic talent which his anxious father tried to fan into genius.

This is an extract from a long poem, in which the Virgin Mary meditates on the terrible knowledge she has that her beautiful baby must one day be sacrificed – a poem that only a mother could write.

From   The Virgin Mary to the Child Jesus
Elizabeth Barratt Browning

Unchildlike shade! – no other babe doth wear
An aspect very sorrowful, as Thou.
No small babe-smiles my watching heart has seen,
To float like speech the speechless lips between:
No dovelike cooing in the golden air,
No quick short joys of leaping babyhood.
Alas, our earthly good,
In heaven thought evil, seems too good for Thee;
Yet, sleep, my weary One!

And then the drear, sharp tongue of prophecy,
With the dread sense of things which shall be done,
Doth smite me inly, like a sword – a sword?
(That 'smites the Shepherd!') then I think aloud
The words 'despised –'rejected' – every word
Recoiling into darkness as I view
The darling on my knee.
Bright angels, move not! lest ye stir the cloud
Betwixt my soul and His futurity!
I must not die, with mother's work to do,
And could not live – and see.

April 4th Easter Sunday

We first visited Clyro, the village forever associated with the Reverend Francis Kilvert one cold, watercolour-grey March day over thirty years ago. Then the village was still small and unspoiled, a tumble of limewashed stone-tiled cottages at the foot of a sweep of hill, the church (not the one Kilvert knew – it was rebuilt after his death) and a few fine houses. Beyond, meadows ran down to the Wye, and the road to Hay, still a quiet grey town. As we arrived, the churchyard was full of women with flowers, dressing the graves for Easter Sunday.

Since then the village has expanded, acquired a hillside of executive bungalows with heather rockeries and a row of town houses. The road now seems busier than it did then, cars and lorries hurtling past. Hay is no longer quiet and grey, but stuffed full of shops selling distressed furniture, olive oils, droopy linens in sage and terracotta, designer jewellery. Oh and still a few bookshops

Francis Kilvert was curate in Clyro for only seven years, between 1865 – 72, but the diaries he wrote there make him undoubtedly its laureate. He wrote with a restless and urgent desire to find the right word, the precise phrase;

I looked out at dawn. The moon was entangled among light clouds in the North and made a golden maze and network across which the slender poplars swayed and bowed themselves with a solemn and measured movement in the west wind..

How many writers would persist beyond describing just the sway of the poplar trees to go on to that 'solemn and measured movement.' ?

For some time, I have been trying to find the right word for the shimmering, glancing, tumbling movement of the poplar trees in the sun and wind. It was 'dazzle'. The dazzle of the poplars.

Another quality of Kilvert's was his genuine love of the local people and his interest in them and their ways (too much interest sometimes, for our comfort, if a pretty girl-child came his way.) His quiet attentiveness to what they said, and did, make vivid little pictures of everyday life in that quiet valley over a hundred years ago.

Read to Sarah Probert, the story of the raising of Lazarus. Hannah came in and sat by the fire listening with grunts of assent between the whiffs of her short pipe. She said she had been 'tugging and tearing firewood up the old dingle.' A squirrel's skin hung over the hearth. The cat killed the squirrel and several others a month ago. 'I couldna think,' said Hannah 'what she was a-tushing down the fold.'

This quotation isn't a poem, and it wasn't written for Easter, but for Quinquagesima Sunday. But it sums up Easter for me, and the joyful feeling of resurrection. And as I read it, I can see the tumbled gravestones beneath the dark flank of hill, and imagine Clyro as it looked to Kilvert.

From Francis Kilvert's Diary

As I walked in the Churchyard this morning the fresh sweet sunny air was full of the singing of the birds and the brightness and gladness of Spring. Some of the graves were white as snow with snowdrops. The southern side of the churchyard was crowded with a multitude of tombstones. They stood thick together, some taller, some short, some looking over the shoulders of others, and as they stood up all looking one way and facing the morning sun they looked like a crowd of men, and it seemed as if the morning of the Resurrection had come and the sleepers had arisen from their graves and were standing upon their feet silent and solemn, all looking towards the East to meet the Rising of the Sun. The whole air was melodious with the distant indefinite sound of sweet bells that seemed to be ringing from every quarter by turns, now from the hill, now from the valley, now from the deer forest, now from the river. The chimes rose and fell, swelled and grew faint again

April 6th

It was a line of Donne's which started it off:

A bracelet of bright haire, about the bone

For some reason those words send shivers down the spine; almost literally; the feeling gathers itself in the back the neck and explodes like a star-burst. It's the 'hairs on the back of the neck' sensation that Housman describes as being essential to true poetry.

Poetry indeed seems to me more physical than intellectual. ...I could no more define poetry than a terrier could define a rat, but experience has taught me, when I am shaving of a morning, to keep watch over my thoughts, because if a line of poetry strays into my memory, my skin bristles so that the razor ceases to act. This particular symptom is accompanied by a shiver down the spine; there is another which consists in a constriction of the throat and a precipitation of water to the eyes; and there is a third which I can only describe by borrowing a phrase from one of Keats' last letters, where he says, speaking of Fanny Brawne, 'everything that reminds me of her goes through me like a spear'.

(*The Name and Nature of Poetry* - lecture given at Cambridge - 1933)

Emily Dickinson says; 'If I feel physically that the top of my head were taken off, I know that is poetry.'

But what is it about the juxtaposition of ordinary words that can do this; how an everyday, commonplace word like 'bone' can suddenly become transformed into something new and strange? It's partly alliteration, the little salvoes of *br* and *b*, but also the picture in your head, golden hair and yellowed bone, beautiful and repulsive together. But something more than this, too.

Other lines that have this effect on me:

Hang there, like fruit my soul, till the tree die...

Cover her face; mine eyes dazzle; she died young

Finish, good lady; the bright day is done
And we are for the dark...

Oh, I'll leap up to my God; who pulls me down?
See see where Christ's blood streams in the firmament...

You and I and Amyas.
Amyas and you and I,
To the greenwood we must go, alas,
You and I, my lyf, and Amyas.

I saw the auld moon late yestreen
With the new moon in her arms...

And this one, a little later, written in time of plague:

Brightness falls from the air
Queens have died young and fair
Dust hath closed Helen's eye;
I am sick, I must die.
Lord have mercy upon us.

This is the spine-tingling song of a young girl on her wedding morning. Surely the anonymous writer was a woman.

The Bailey Beareth the Bell Away   Anon (15th century)

The maidens came
When I was in my mother's bower;
I had all that I would
The bailey beareth the bell away;
The lily, the rose, the rose I lay,
The silver is white, red is the gold;
The robes they lay in fold.
The bailey beareth the bell away;
The lily, the rose, the rose I lay.
And through the glass window shines the sun.
How should I love, and I so young?
The bailey beareth the bell away;
The lily, the rose, the rose I lay.

April 9th

Here's just a fragment from one of the most beautiful medieval poems, *Quia Amore Langueo*, Christ's lament, written as though a lover, for the human soul who has betrayed him.

From   Quia Amore Langueo   Anon (15th Century)

I am treulove that fals was never;
My sistur, mannys soule, I loved hyr thus;
By-cause I wold on no wyse disseuere,
I left my kingdom gloriouse;

I purveyed hyr a place full preciouse,
She flytt, I folowyd, I luffed her soo
That I suffred these paynès piteouse
Quia amore langueo....

I crowned hyr with blysse and she me with thorne,
I led hyr to chamber and she me to dye,
I browght hir to worship and she me to skorne,
I did her reverence and she me velanye.
To love that loveth is no maistrye,
Hyr hate made never my love hyr foo;
Ask then no more questions whye
But *Quia amore langueo*

April 10th

Hairs on the back of the neck and shivers down the spine... Music or words? Is it either/or? I like music, but probably if it wasn't there I wouldn't miss it. But I wouldn't like to live without words, without stories, without poetry.

Perhaps you can have both. Proust uses the famous 'little phrase' of the imaginary composer Vinteuil, to set off a volley of associations. It reminds Swann of his love for Odette every time he hears it; it becomes one of their secret codes. So the music is about both itself and its erotic associations. Proust scholars have expended much time and energy trying to guess what the real-life original of the 'little phrase' was – I don't think it matters. *Heard melodies are sweet/ but those unheard are sweeter.*

Here is Swann, coming to Odette's little house, listening to the 'little phrase' which worked its magic, even though, and perhaps because, Odette doesn't play well:

He would rap upon the pane, and she would hear the signal, and answer, before running to meet him at the gate. He would find, lying open on the piano, some of her favourite music, the Valse des Roses, the Pauvre Fou of Tagliafico (which, according to the instructions embodied in her will, was to be played at her funeral); but he would ask her, instead, to give him the little phrase from Vinteuil's sonata. It was true that Odette played vilely, but often the fairest impression that remains in our minds of a favourite air is one that has arisen out of a jumble of wrong notes struck by unskilful fingers upon a tuneless piano. The little phrase was associated still in Swann's mind, with his love for Odette.

(From Swann in Love - Marcel Proust – tr Scott Moncrieff)

Richard is the family musical person, and so I asked him for his four spine-tingling pieces of music. He came up with these;

Handel:	*Waft her angels (Jephtha.)*
Schubert:	*String quintet in C major.*
Ravel:	*Pavane pour une infante defunte.*
Macmillan:	*Strathclyde motets.*

This poem ties words and music together. It might or might not be by Shakespeare: it was first printed by a literary pirate in *The Passionate Pilgrim* along with a lot of stuff that wasn't. I think it sounds like the young Shakespeare, written in the first flush of passion for his lovely boy. (I'm for that boy being the Earl of Southampton, partly because of that portrait of him painted when he was in the Tower with his cat. Anyone who likes cats has my vote.)

If Music and Sweet Poetry   Anon

If music and sweet poetry agree,
As they must needs, the sister and the brother,
Then must the love be great 'twixt thee and me,
Because thou lov'st the one, and I the other.
Dowland to thee is dear, whose heavenly touch
Upon the lute doth ravish human sense;
Spenser to me, whose deep conceit is such
As, passing all conceit, needs no defence.
Thou love'st to hear the sweet melodious sound,
That Phoebus' lute, the queen of music makes:
And I in deep delight am chiefly drown'd
Whenas himself to singing he betakes.
One god is god of both, as poets feign:
One knight loves both, and both in thee remain.

April 14th

A London dinner party in 1818, Wordsworth, eminent and middle-aged, is holding forth on some topic or other. An ardent young man is so excited that he tries to break in on the monologue with an observation of his own; whereupon, the great poet's wife lays a warning hand on his arm, and says, severely: 'Mr Wordsworth is never interrupted.' Oh, how you long, across the years, to grab her by the shoulder and hiss into her ear 'But that's Keats, Mrs W, you pillock! *Keats!*'

Keats' letters are wonderful bedside reading, as his pen ' gleans his teeming brain'; seldom do you see a mind like his running at full tilt along, breathless but in control, bawdy, profound and gossipy:

(Devonshire) *is a splashy, rainy, misty snowy, foggy, haily, floody, muddy, slipshod country – the hills are very beautiful when you get a sight of 'em- the Primroses are out, but then you are in...*

And then the heartbreaking last words of the last letter, written from Rome, where he'd gone in what he must have known was a doomed attempt to regain his health; *I can scarcely bring myself to say farewell, even in a letter : I always made an awkward bow...*

I chose this poem because of words running through my head last night; in the morning, I found them in the sonnet 'Bright Star', which he wrote on a blank page in a book of Shakespeare's poems, and which was published posthumously.

Bright Star   John Keats

Bright star, would I were stedfast as thou art –
Not in lone splendour hung aloft the night
And watching with eternal lids apart
Like nature's patient, sleepless Eremite,
The moving waters at their priestlike task
Of pure ablution round earth's human shores,
Or gazing on the new soft-fallen mask
Of snow upon the mountains and the moors –
Not – yet still stedfast, still unchangeable,
Pillow'd upon my fair love's ripening breast,
To feel for ever its soft fall and swell,
Awake for ever in a sweet unrest,
Still, still to hear her tender-taken breath,
And so live ever – or else swoon to death

April 15th

We're travelling into Shrewsbury today. Shrewsbury – Shropshire, so one obvious voice. Only I was disappointed one day, going to Worcestershire , to find that Bredon Hill isn't even in Shropshire at all. And that 'Shropshire' – those 'blue remembered hills' – wasn't part of his own poetic memories, but simply chosen as a location because it sounds evocative.

Never mind; Shropshire is a beautiful county, with its mazy little lanes, sudden hills and steep valleys, its velvety greens; a kind of Wales in miniature.

I particularly like the third verse of this poem, the beech-leaves 'staining' the wind, the 'burnish' of the grasses; and 'heaves' ostensibly there to rhyme with the more predictable 'sheaves' but how precisely right for the slow, heavy movement of the long grass gone to seed, beneath the wind

Tell me not here, it needs not saying   A.E. Housman

Tell me not here, it needs not saying,
What tune the enchantress plays
In aftermaths of soft September
Or under blanching mays,
For she and I were long acquainted
And I knew all her ways.

On russet floors, by waters idle,
The pine lets fall its cone:
The cuckoo shouts all day at nothing
In leafy dells alone;

And traveller's joy beguiles in autumn
Hearts that have lost their own.

On acres of the seeded grasses
The changing burnish heaves:
Or marshalled under moons of harvest
Stands still all night the sheaves:
Or beeches strip in storms for winter
And stain the wind with leaves.

Possess, as I possessed a season,
The countries I resign,
Where over elmy plains the highway
Would mount the hills and shine,
And full of shade the pillared forest
Would murmur and be mine.
For nature, heartless, witless nature,
Will neither care nor know
What stranger's feel may find the meadow
And trespass there and go,
Nor ask amid the dews of morning
If they are mine or no.

April 16th

Nature, 'heartless, witless Nature' wins out again, as a volcano in far-away Iceland has managed to bring the entire air transport system of Western Europe and America to a halt. Planes are stranded, passengers sit helplessly on piles of luggage, the air is thick with invisible toxic particles, it's nobody's fault, and nobody knows what will happen next.

The volcano made me think of Hell, the fiery depths, the unutterable punishment. Volcanoes, with their strange moon-landscapes, choking dust, sulphurous smells, dangerous fissures, and glimpses of that violent, raging crimson core, are hell beneath our feet, always lurking , ready to trap us.

Milton ('a true poet and of the Devil's party' as Blake says) is perhaps the English poet who has thought most about hell, its landscapes, its hierarchies. Here's Satan, the undoubted star of *Paradise Lost*, in sonorous, splendid blank verse:

From   **Paradise Lost**   **John Milton**

Him the Almighty Power
Hurld headlong flaming from th'Ethereal Skie
With hideous ruine and combustion down
To bottomless perdition, there to dwell
In Adamantine chains and penal Fire
Who durst defie th'Omnipotent to Arms.
Nine times the Space that measures day and Night
To mortal men, he with his horrid crew
Lay vanquisht, rowling in the fiery Gulfe,
Confounded though immortal: But his doom
Reserv'd him to more wrath; for now the thought
Both of lost happiness and lasting pain
Torments him; round he throws his baleful eyes
That witness'd huge affliction and dismay
Mixt with obdurate pride and stedfast hate:

At once as far as Angels kenn he views
The dismal situation waste and wilde
A Dungeon horrible, on all sides round
As one great Furnace flam'd, yet from those flames
No light, but rather darkness visible
Serv'd only to discover sights of woe
Regions of sorrow, doleful shades, where peace
And rest can never dwell, hope never comes
That comes to all...

April 17th

We have three eminent biographers coming to lunch today, and we try to decide what the collective noun for biographers is. A Whisper of Biographers? An Insinuation of Biographers? A Gossip of Biographers? No, that's not fair. A Revelation of Biographers? An Affirmation of Biographers?

I ask our friend Paul Ferris, who as well as the definitive biography of Dylan Thomas, has written many novels and much journalism – more words than is almost humanly possible. In his novels, he delights in the strange underside of respectable British life, the quirks and idiosyncrasies, the hypocrisies and subterfuges. I asked him for a poem, and he suggested this by Yeats. But no heaven's embroidered cloths or bean rows; here is one of Yeats's later and darker poems, straight from *the foul rag and bone shop of the heart.*

Who was John Kinsella? Who was Mary Moore? I'm irritated by Yeats's habit of dropping in names you don't know, references you don't have, as though his poetry is an esoteric game to which you aren't invited. It's an elegy, for the death of a brothel keeper, by an old man, who feels his last chance for sexual pleasure has died with her. Her drunken stories —*not for the priest's ear*- were such that they *kept his soul alive.* It's the hidden Ireland that subverts the priests, finds pleasure in the paradoxical, the stubborn, the rebel, the profaner, the disobedient. It's life-affirming in a curious way, yet not one for feminists, I think

John Kinsella's Lament for Mrs Mary Moore   W.B. Yeats

A bloody and a sudden end,
    Gunshot or a noose,
For Death who takes what man would keep,
    Leaves what man would lose.
He might have had my sister,
    My cousins by the score,
But nothing satisfied the fool
    But my dear Mary Moore,
None other knows what pleasures man
    At table or in bed.
What shall I do for pretty girls
    Now my old bawd is dead?

Though stiff to strike a bargain,
    Like an old Jew man,
Her bargain struck we laughed and talked
    And emptied many a can;
And O! but she had stories,
    Though not for the priest's ear,

To keep the soul of man alive,
    Banish age and care,
And being old she put a skin
    On everything she said,
What shall I do for pretty girls
    Now my old bawd is dead?

The priests have got a book that says
    But for Adam's sin
Eden's garden would be there
    And I there within.
No expectation fails there,
    No pleasing habit ends,
No man grows old, no girl grows cold,
    But friends walk by friends.
Who quarrels over halfpennies
    That plucks the tree for bread?
What shall I do for pretty girls
    Now my old bawd is dead?

April 19th

Yesterday's poem led me to look again at the later poems of Yeats; some irritatingly obscure, some bawdy, some deeply moving. The use of the refrain anchors many of these poems, sometimes oddly, sometimes beautifully. And I found one of my favourite poems, having forgotten it was there. It tells of the supreme concentration which must lie behind any great movement or idea.

Long-legged Fly   W.B. Yeats

That civilisation may not sink,
Its great battle lost,
Quiet the dog, tether the pony
To a distant post;
Our master Caesar is in the tent
Where the maps are spread,
His eyes fixed upon nothing,
A hand under his head.
Like a long-legged fly upon the stream
His mind moves upon silence.

That the topless towers be burnt
And men recall that face,
Move most slowly if move you must
In this lonely place.
She thinks, part woman, three parts a child,
That no-body looks; her feet
Practise a tinker shuffle
Picked up on a street.
Like a long-legged fly upon the stream
Her mind moves upon silence.

That girls at puberty may find
The first Adam in their thought,
Shut the door of the Pope's chapel,
Keep those children out.
There on the scaffolding reclines

Michael Angelo,
With no more sound than the mice make
His hand moves to and fro.
Like a long legged fly upon the stream
His mind moves upon silence

April 26th

Off to Lambeth today, and bright Spring sunshine in which to walk
along the South Bank trying to imagine the marshy duck-haunted
village that Lambeth was in William Blake's day. Although even
then, the factories were encroaching – the 'satanic' ruins of the
great Albion Flour mills, burned down in 1791, dominated the
riverside. Blake lived for some years in Hercules Buildings, and
often surprised his neighbours by sitting naked in the summer
house with his wife reading Paradise Lost. It's also where he saw
the angel Gabriel, one evening while he was muttering about the
impossibility of drawing an angel. 'Who can paint an angel?' he
said. A voice came from behind him 'Michelangelo could.' He
turned to see his study flooded with light. 'And how do you know?'
he said, for he was used to talking to angels. 'I *know,*' went on the
voice 'for I sat for him. I am the archangel Gabriel.' But Blake
needed to be convinced. 'Oho! You are, are you? I must have better
assurance of that than a wandering voice. You may be an evil spirit
– there are such in this land.' 'You shall have good assurance,'
replied the archangel. 'Can an evil spirit do *this?*' And the light grew
brighter, the roof of Blake's study opened to the skies, the spirit
ascended, and there 'moved the universe.' Blake was persuaded.

I used to teach in Lambeth years ago: and loved the names of the streets; Black Prince Road, Paradise Row, Lollard Street. Hercules Buildings had long gone, but there were tenements all along Hercules Road. A pupil of mine, Oliver, lived in those tenements. He had been brought up in St Lucia, by his grandmother; she had died and he had at first gone to live in Canada with relatives. He was happy in Canada and his relatives wanted him to stay, but his mother was living in London and she had summoned him to live with her. Oliver was a small boy with a huge smile, and great enthusiasm for everything. Blake would have liked him for his innocence and joy. His mother was a religious fanatic and I think probably clinically mad. Oliver's wide smile stiffened slightly. The other boys, especially those from Jamaican backgrounds, despised him; Oliver was not cool. They called him 'jungle bunny'. The smile grew bewildered. Soon he started retaliating. The smile was still there on occasions, but now another expression was taking its place. A Song of Innocence was fast becoming a Song of Experience. I often wonder what happened to him after I left.

Today Lambeth is full of smart flats and businesses, flowers spill from window boxes and planters, the tenements have gone or been gentrified.

I like this poem by Blake; I like the precision of his mystical geography, and I love it that he used the real London as the location of his visionary Jerusalem. Every time I travel back to Wales, I whisper 'mournful, ever-weeping Paddington' to myself beneath the great arched glass roof of that noisy, busy station.

His fascination with 'druids' as representing the ancient, but gruesome past of 'Albion' was influenced by mad Iolo Morganwg, who held the first modern Gorsedd on Primrose Hill in 1792. Everything, new and ancient, real and visionary, was linked in a dazzling network; everything resonated with layers of meaning upon meaning. He was the most magical of poets, and the most London-centred.

From **Jerusalem** **William Blake**

The fields from Islington to Marybone
    To Primrose Hill and Saint John's Wood,
Were builded over with pillars of gold;
    And there Jerusalem's pillars stood.

Her Little Ones ran on the fields,
    The lamb of God among them seen,
And fair Jerusalem, His Bride,
    Among the little meadows green.

Pancras and Kentish Town repose
    Among her golden pillars high,
Among her golden arches which
    Shine upon the starry sky.

The Jew's-harp House and the Green Man,
    The Ponds where boys to bathe delight,
The fields of cows by William's farm,
    Shine in Jerusalem's pleasant sight.

She walks upon our meadows green;
　　The Lamb of God walks by her side;
And every English child is seen,
　　Children of Jesus and his Bride;

Forgiving trespasses and sins,
　　Lest Babylon, with cruel Og,
With Moral and Self-righteous Law,
　　Should crucify in Satan's Synagogue.

What are those Golden Builders doing
　　Near mournful ever-weeping Paddington,
Standing above that mighty ruin,
　　Where Satan the first victory won;

Where Albion slept beneath the fatal Tree,
　　And the Druid's golden knife
Rioted in human gore,
　　In offerings of Human Life?

April 27th

The cherry trees are out in Hoxton, laden with curds of white blossom. I don't like the pink trees; they're too sugary for me, but I enjoy the white ones. *Lovliest of trees….*I find myself murmuring.

Then I look at the name of the estate opposite me. And it's Wenlock Barn….

So only one poem will do today, though really it's too well known. Probably the cherry tree that Housman saw was the delicate wild bird cherry, not the thick fondant swirls of the ornamental trees. We have some in our Welsh garden; for eleven months, useless spindly things, ready for the chop. But then once a year they burst into starry blossom.

The words of the poem have bitten into my brain – I can't see cherry trees in Spring without whispering them to myself; remembering how when I first heard them, I too had only used up twenty of my three-score years and ten....

Loveliest of Trees   A.E. Housman

Loveliest of trees, the cherry now
Is hung with bloom along the bough,
And stands about the woodland ride
Wearing white for Eastertide.

Now of my threescore years and ten
Twenty will not come again,
And take from seventy springs a score,
It only leaves me fifty more.

And since to look at things in bloom
Fifty springs are little room,
About the woodland I will go
To see the cherry hung with snow.

April 28th

Another poem that seems too well known. But I realised that I'd never read beyond the first two famous lines. Well, the daffodils are passing away, and it's such a graceful, delicate little poem I can't resist it.

To Daffodils   Robert Herrick

Fair daffodils, we weep to see
    You haste away so soon:
As yet the early-rising Sun
    Has not attain'd his noon.

    Stay, stay
Until the hasting day
    Has run
But to the even-song;
And having pray'd together, we
    Will go with you along.

We have short time to stay, as you,
    We have as short a Spring;
As quick a growth to meet decay
    As you, or anything.
    We die,
As your hours do, and dry
    Away
Like to the Summer's rain;
Or as the pearls of morning dew,
    Ne'er to be found again.

May

May 1st

Poets have found a good deal to say about May, the start of summer, the symbol of blooming youth as opposed to withered age. Here's Samuel Daniel, in one of his beautiful sequence of sonnets addressed to Delia. The theme is the usual one, the poet urging the bashful woman that she'd better sleep with him now while she still has her looks, since when she's old and wrinkled no-one will want her. But it's charmingly done here, I think.

From   **Sonnets to Delia**   **Samuel Daniel**

But love whilst that thou mayst be loved again,
  Now whilst thy May hath filled thy lap with flowers,
Now whilst thy beauty bears without a stain;
  Now use the summer smiles ere winter lours.
And whilst thou spread'st unto the rising sun
  The fairest flower that ever saw the light,
Now joy thy time before thy sweet be done:
  And, Delia, think thy morning must have night,
And that thy brightness sets at length to west,
  When thou wilt close up that which now thou show'st;
And think the same becomes thy fading best,
  Which then shall most enveil and shadow most.
    Men do not weigh the stalk for that it was,
    When once they find her flower, her glory, pass.

May 6th

Well, Election Day is here at last and now we're waiting to see if it's to be the Tin Man, the Scarecrow or the Cowardly Lion. By this time tomorrow we'll know the worst.

Here's a picture of a smooth operator (actually the rebellious Duke of Monmouth) working the crowd:

From   Absalom and Achitophel   John Dryden

Impatient of high hopes, urg'd with renown
And Fir'd with near possession of a Crown.
The admiring Croud are dazzled with surprize
And on his goodly person feast their eyes:
His joy conceal'd, he sets himself to show:
On each side bowing popularly low:
His looks, his gestures, and his words he frames
And with familiar ease repeats their Names.
Thus form'd by Nature, furnished out with Arts
He glides unfelt into their secret hearts…

May 10th

Still we don't have a government and none of the choices will make anyone happy. Everyone wants to climb on the platform, and no-one's quite sure how to do it. Ulysses, the wily anti-hero of Shakespeare's Troilus and Cressida has fame and fortune pretty well sussed out, as he explains to Achilles, in his famous speech. Do it now, seize the moment, or everyone will forget you.

From **Troilus and Cressida Act iii sc 3 William Shakespeare**

Time hath, my lord, a wallet at his back,

Wherein he puts alms for oblivion,

A great-sized monster of ingratitudes:

Those scraps are good deeds past; which are devour'd

As fast as they are made, forgot as soon

As done: perseverance, dear my lord,

Keeps honour bright: to have done is to hang

Quite out of fashion, like a rusty mail

In monumental mockery. Take the instant way;

For honour travels in a strait so narrow,

Where one but goes abreast: keep then the path;

For emulation hath a thousand sons

That one by one pursue: if you give way,

Or hedge aside from the direct forthright,

Like to an enter'd tide, they all rush by

And leave you hindmost;

Or like a gallant horse fall'n in first rank,

Lie there for pavement to the abject rear,

O'er-run and trampled on: then what they do in present,

Though less than yours in past, must o'ertop yours;

For time is like a fashionable host

That slightly shakes his parting guest by the hand,

And with his arms outstretch'd, as he would fly,

Grasps in the comer: welcome ever smiles,

And farewell goes out sighing. O, let not virtue seek

Remuneration for the thing it was;

For beauty, wit,

High birth, vigour of bone, desert in service,
Love, friendship, charity, are subjects all
To envious and calumniating time.
One touch of nature makes the whole world kin,
That all with one consent praise new-born gawds,
Though they are made and moulded of things past,
And give to dust that is a little gilt
More laud than gilt o'er-dusted.
The present eye praises the present object.
Then marvel not, thou great and complete man,
That all the Greeks begin to worship Ajax;
Since things in motion sooner catch the eye
Than what not stirs.

May 14th

Just one last day among politics. This is John Cleveland's Epitaph on the Earl of Strafford. Thomas Wentworth, Earl of Strafford, started off his public life as a reluctant Parliamentarian, who stood up for the rights of Parliament and the people against the king, and was even imprisoned briefly. Later on, though, he took up the cause of the King with complete enthusiasm, and as Lord Deputy of Ireland, ran a brutal and oppressive policy. Parliament turned against him when he facilitated the King's unpopular and unsuccessful war against the Scots; he was tried for High Treason, and though case against him was unclear, condemned to death. Charles' decision to sign the condemnation weighed heavily on him for the rest of his life; he even considered his own execution may have been a punishment for it.

Strafford seems to have been a driven and obsessed man. His second wife died after he'd forced her to travel when pregnant, and her family blamed him for it. His portrait shows a bulldog expression, dark unsmiling eyes beneath heavy brows, though his conversation could be light and witty. He said 'I am not afraid of death, but do as cheerfully put off my doublet at this time as ever I did when I went to bed.' Nick Clegg's loyalty to his new master won't meet such an end as Strafford's, but loyalty can be a dangerous thing in politics.

This afternoon we hope to plant apple trees; Ribstone Pippins, Red Falstaff, Winter Gem.

Epitaph on the Earl of Strafford   John Cleveland

Here lies wise and valiant dust,
Huddled up 'twixt fit and juste:
Strafford, who was hurried hence
'Twixt treason and convenience.
He spent his time here in a mist,
A *Papist* yet a *Calvinist;*
His Prince's nearest joy and Grief:
He had, yet wanted , all relief;
The Prop and Ruine of the State,
The peoples violent love and hate,
One in extremes lov'd and abhorr'd.
Riddles lie here, or in a word,
Here lies blood, and let it lie
Speechlesse still, and never cry.

May 24th

Elizabeth Bagueley belongs to a group of writers for children to which I also belong . She's a story teller as well as a writer; I learn from what she's written about herself that she recites poetry aloud which embarrasses her children. 'Knowing poetry,' she says 'makes life a better place,' and I have to agree with her.

She's suggested many lovely poems to me; among them, this by Dante Gabriel Rossetti. Some of his poems, like his later paintings, can be overblown and florid, but I love the enigmatic simplicity of this poem of loss and grief, the delicate touch of it:

The Woodspurge   Dante Gabriel Rossetti

The wind flapped loose, the wind was still:
Shaken out dead from tree and hill:
I had walked on at the wind's will, -
I sat now, for the wind was still.

Between my knees my forehead was, -
My lips, drawn in, said not Alas!
My hair was over in the grass,
My naked ears heard the day pass.

My eyes, wide open, had the run
Of some ten weeds to fix upon;
Among those few, out of the sun,
The woodspurge flowered, three cups in one.

From perfect grief there need not be
Wisdom or even memory:
One thing then learnt remains to me, -
The woodspurge has a cup of three.

May 28th

This morning I had a beautiful drift of yellow poppies against our stone wall, wild but carefully cultivated by me over the years. I turn my back for ten minutes to find them all gone, ripped out, every feathery leaf, every shimmering petal, every last seedling, swept away by the tarmac men.

I thought of William Cowper, poor, fragile, melancholy William Cowper, who kept afloat by leading a life of blameless and cheerful domesticity with his beloved Mrs Unwin, trying to fend off the awful religious gloom that engulfed him periodically. The first lines of his poem about Alexander Selkirk *I am monarch of all I survey...'* are usually quoted as an example of cheery gung-ho – they are anything but.

One day he found his favourite spinney cut down, and wrote mournfully about it to a friend: *'last night at nine o clock we entered [the spinney] for the first time this summer. We had not walked many yards in it before we perceived that this pleasant retreat is destined never to be a pleasant retreat again. In one more year, the whole will be a thicket. That which was once the serpentine walk is now in a state of transformation and is already become as woody as the rest. Poplars and elms without number are springing in the turf; they are now as high as the knee....the desolation of the whole scene is such, that it sunk our spirits. The ponds are dry; the circular one in front of the hermitage is filled with flags and rushes........the ivy and the moss , with which the hermitage was lined, are torn away…. So farewell, Spinney. I have promised myself I will never enter it again….*

The Poplar Field   William Cowper

The poplars are fell'd: farewell to the shade
And the whispering sound of the cool colonnade;
The winds play no longer and sing in the leaves,
Nor Ouse on his bosom their image receives.

Twelve years have elapsed since I first took a view
Of my favourite field, and the bank where they grew:
And now in the grass behold they are laid,
And the tree is my seat that once lent me a shade.

The blackbird has fled to another retreat,
Where the hazels afford him a screen from the heat:
And the scene where his melody charm'd me before
Resounds with his sweet-flowing ditty no more .

My fugitive years are all hasting away,
And I must ere long lie as lowly as they,
With a turf on my breast and a stone at my head,
Ere another such grove shall arise in its stead.

'Tis a sight to engage me, if anything can,
To muse on the perishing pleasures of man;
Though his life be a dream, his enjoyments, I see,
Have a being less durable even than he.

May 29th

Today's poem is also about desolation and loss, though on a far more epic and tragic scale than Cowper's poplars or my poppies. We have friends staying with us for the Hay Festival, Colin and Sarah Tucker; Colin's a writer, script editor and film director, and he suggested this, from the old black-and-lemon Penguin book of American verse.

Vachel Lindsay was an oddball; his parents wanted him to be a doctor, but he became a poet, a big, strange shambling person, who later sank into melancholy and committed suicide by poison. But he's one of that generation of poets who were deliberately looking for a distinct American voice, fresh, spare and modern.

Any sensitive traveller in the States must be aware, if only through the names of the towns and villages, of that huge lost population of men and beasts; this poem is heart-breaking, but I'm pleased to have found it.

The Flower-fed Buffaloes   Vachel Lindsay

The flower-fed buffaloes of the spring
In the days of long ago,
Ranged where the locomotives sing
And the prairie flowers lie low:-
The tossing, blooming perfumed grass
Is swept away by the wheat,
Wheels and wheels and wheels spin by
In the spring that still is sweet.
But the flower-fed buffaloes of the spring
Left us, long ago.

They gore no more, they bellow no more,
They trundle around the hills no more:-
With the Blackfeet, lying low,
With the Pawnees, lying low
Lying low.

June

June 2nd

After the pale and pallid post-winter , one of the most beautiful days I ever remember, though as we're looking out on saturated green hills, in another beautiful area, the Lake District, a madman is running amok with a gun and killing people.

We're taking visitors on a tour of our three local churches, all in circular pre-Christian sites, all dedicated to St David, *Dewi Sant*. We're looking at bluebell slopes, washed with intensest violet, meadows glazed with buttercups, hedgerows frothing with cow parsley and red campion. A cuckoo seems to follow us through the valley, calling loudly and clearly. There don't seem to be bluebell poems, for some reason. I suppose they make bad poems, just as, on the whole, they make for terrible paintings and photographs. You do better with cuckoos, *singing lhude; but a wandering voice ; whose note full many a man doth mark*

But you don't walk far among these hills without the constant company of skylarks, the song stretched out in a shimmer of sound from horizon to horizon, one bird taking up the melody as another leaves off. This is one of those seemingly simple poems that seems freighted with hidden meaning, just as those unseen singers accompany you through the bracken. Although Rossetti loved nature, and wrote eloquently about it, she was a lifetime city-dweller, and much of her nature poetry has an air of exile and exclusion about it. It's been attractively set to music by Michael Head.

A Green Cornfield   Christina Rossetti

'And singing still dost soar and soaring ever singest.'

The earth was green, the sky was blue:
　　I saw and heard one sunny morn
A skylark hang between the two,
　　A singing speck above the corn;

A stage below, in gay accord,
　　White butterflies danced on the wing,
And still the singing skylark soared,
　　And silent sank and soared to sing.

The cornfield stretched a tender green
　　To right and left beside my walks;
I knew he had a nest unseen
　　Somewhere among the million stalks.

And as I paused to hear his song
　　While swift the sunny moments slid,
Perhaps his mate sat listening long,
　　And listened longer than I did.

June 6th

Another skylark poem. Today is the last day of the Hay Festival. Soon the tented city will be folded away, the crowds depart, the posters and the flags taken down, the meadows go back to buttercups and sheep and Hay reverts to its usual state of being a small market town with pretensions. But we aren't in Hay today.

Instead we go for a walk on the hill, the peace only broken once by a group of lads on motorbikes. Larks still trill endlessly in the background. We recently heard a beautiful performance by Marcia Crayford of Vaughan Williams's *Lark Ascending* . But the poem that inspired him isn't so well known. It's by George Meredith, and though I think it's a bit too long and too breathless, it's a fine poem. I won't quote it all here, just the first part.

From   The Lark Ascending   George Meredith

He rises and begins to round,
He drops the silver chain of sound
Of many links without a break,
In chirrup, whistle, slur and shake,
All intervolv'd and spreading wide,
Like water dimples down a tide
Where ripple ripple overcurls
And eddy into eddy whirls;
A press of hurried notes that run
So fleet they scarce are more than one,
Yet changingly the trills repeat
And linger ringing while they fleet......

June 9th

I've often walked past the church of St Giles in the Fields, behind the windy wasteland of Centre Point, on the way to Tottenham Court Road. Two hundred years ago this was the centre of London's worst slums, the Rookeries, with Gin Lane and all its horrors, Dickens' world of crossing-sweepers and beggars.

I don't know if the 'fields' were still apparent in Shakespeare's day, but the Angel pub, next to St Giles was where those making the long and painful journey to Tyburn would stop and be given a free mug of ale; the St Giles Bowl. Both fields and slums have long gone, but St Giles still has something of the air of a country church. I didn't know, though, that somewhere in its churchyard lies George Chapman, translator of Homer, who died in poverty. Andrew Marvell is buried there, too.

Today in Wales is one of those days where the rain never seems to end. Miserable sodden sheep huddle in the meadows, 'standing on a sixpence' as the farmers call it. Water streams down the road like a river.

All this took me back to Keats, Chapman and the Odyssey, and Ulysses clambering out from the sea which had 'soaked his heart through'. Ulysses has just escaped on a raft from the island of Calypso with the usual mixture of help and hindrance from the gods. Poseidon has spotted him and sends a storm which rages for two days. Finally Ulysses struggles to land, soon to confront the young girl Nausicaa. It's gritty, sinewy poetry, and you feel the heft of Ulysses' endless struggle with the elements; try reading it out loud.

From The Odyssey, Book Five   Homer, translated by George Chapman

Then forth he came, his both knees falt'ring, both
His strong hands hanging down, and all with froth
His cheeks and nosthrils flowing, voice and breath
Spent to all use, and down he sunk to death.
The sea had soak'd his heart through; all his veins

His toils had rack'd t' a labouring woman's pains.
Dead weary was he. But when breath did find
A pass reciprocal, and in his mind
 His spirit was recollected, up he rose,
And from his neck did th' amulet unloose,
That Ino gave him; which he hurl'd from him
To sea. It sounding fell, and back did swim
With th' ebbing waters, till it straight arriv'd
Where Ino's fair hand it again receiv'd.
Then kiss'd he th' humble earth; and on he goes,
Till bulrushes show'd place for his repose…

June 17th

We had to do a lot of needlework at school, and as a clumsy child, I was hopeless at it. My tray cover or matinee jacket would be a mess of wonky uneven blood-spattered stitches, and I had to hope that a kind and nimble-fingered girl would take pity on me and finish the thing off. So it's rather odd that I chose to go to the Quilt Exhibition at the V & A, and odder still that I enjoyed it. Some of the early quilts are exquisite, cotton and silk stitched so close and fine that they gleam like sheets of burnished gold, patterns so intricate and colour schemes so subtle as to be almost incredible.

And yet as you think of all these nameless women, dutifully stitching away as though their lives depended upon it, there's something very sad there. Not all the quilts are by women; one of the most moving is produced by prisoners in Wandsworth jail. In most cases, there's some sort of confinement involved: one is made by prisoners aboard a convict ship, another by women in a

Japanese internment camp, another by a profoundly injured soldier from the Napoleonic wars.

After I leave the V&A I find myself on a number 19 bus in Tottenham Court Road; so on an impulse I jump off, and dive through little back streets to find St Giles, which I wrote about the other day. It's as I remember it, except for a huge new building apparently made of red-and-yellow Lego springing up beside it. I discover that originally St Giles was a leper hospital, founded by Queen Matilda. Also that many of those executed at Tyburn were buried there, including eleven Roman Catholic martyrs. Inside the church, three elderly people are gathered for a Communion service. I hear a strange noise, and nearly fall over a homeless man fast asleep by the wall and snoring like a walrus. I trip over another by Andrew Marvell's memorial stone, but I also find Chapman's memorial. Two of Shelley's children and sad little Allegra Byron were christened here.

The quilts and the thought of those hours spent stitching made me remember some lines from the nearly marvellous *Aurora Leigh*

From   Aurora Leigh Book I   Elizabeth Barratt Browning

We sew, sew, prick our fingers, dull our sight,
Producing what? A pair of slippers, sir,
To put on when you're weary – or a stool
To stumble over and vex you... 'curse that stool!'
Or else at best, a cushion, where you lean
And sleep, and dream of something we are not
But would be for your sake....

June 18th

Sometimes only a poem will do, and if there isn't one out there, you have to be the one to do it. Which is my only excuse for the following:

On the Road From Oxford

The colours have gone crazy this year;
All the flowers have broken out.
On the road from Oxford, we gasp
At the blaze and dazzle of them:
At a meadow gilded with buttercups,
Or blue with a sky-haze of flax.
But it's the poppies that startle.
Imagine, field after field drenched in scarlet!
A bolt of red silk billowed out in an Indian shop,
Or mist of pure pigment hurled by a mad painter;
The whole field flushed and glowing,
So hot, demanding our entire attention,
As if to remind us
That beneath the earth there is fire,
Beneath the skin, there is blood.

June 21st

Belinda Hollyer is a writer who has also edited poetry anthologies, so she's immersed in poems. She writes 'Poetry supports, informs and gladdens my life at every level.' She said it would be hard to chose 'The One.' I suggested instead she choose 'The Several' – and here is one of The Several. A favourite of mine, too; this haunting poem by Hardy, which always comes to mind on those strange and poignant moments when someone long dead briefly flares into life again in the face of a living sibling.

Heredity   Thomas Hardy

I am the family face;
Flesh perishes, I live on,
Projecting trait and trace
Through time to times anon,
And leaping from place to place
Over oblivion.

The years-heired feature that can
In curve and voice and eye
Despise the human span
Of durance – that is I:
The eternal thing in man,
That heeds no call to die.

June 22nd

Eric and Marlene Hobsbawm have a country cottage not far from here, and when Marlene learned that I was 'collecting' poems, she sent me an inspirational one, Primo Levi's *To My Friends*. Both Eric and Marlene are people who are especially good at friendship, so I've found another on the same subject.

This is a mournful, elegiac one, though. Letitia Elizabeth Landon, now forgotten, was a prolific and successful poet in her day, and supported a rather importunate family by her pen alone.

Once she attracted some scandal or other, and perhaps to escape, she contracted an unfortunate marriage to George Maclean, governor of what was then the Gold Coast. Shortly after her arrival, she was found dead, possibly by murder, possibly suicide, probably fever. She was thirty-six.

On her sea journey to Africa, she wrote this melancholy poem about her never-to-be-seen-again friends, which elicited poetic replies from both Elizabeth Barratt Browning and Christina Rossetti.

From **The Ocean – Night at Sea**
Letitia Elizabeth Landon 'L.E.L'

By each dark wave around the vessel sweeping,
Farther am I from dear old friends removed;
Till the lone vigil that I now am keeping
I did not know how much you were beloved.
How many acts of kindness little heeded,
Kind looks, kind words, rise half reproachful now!
Hurried and anxious, my vexed life has speeded,
And memory wears a soft accusing brow.
My friends, my absent friends!
Do you think of me, as I think of you?
The very stars are strangers, as I catch them
Athwart the shadowy sails that swell above;
I cannot hope that other eyes will watch them
At the same moment with a mutual love.
They shine not there, as here they now are shining:
The very hours are changed. – Ah, do ye sleep?
O'er each home pillow midnight is declining –

May some kind dream at least my image keep!
My friends, my absent friends!
Do you think of me, as I think of you?

July

July 5th

I don't know why this poem chose itself today, but it came into my mind. Maybe because I've been thinking about the vagaries of memory, especially as you get older. Browning muses on meeting someone who had met Shelley. Shelley, who had died when Browning was ten, was his idol. And yet this unnamed person seems immune to the memory of the great man; the memory isn't important to him, it's simply one he has among many others.

And then the poem goes off at an unexpected tangent ; you think Browning will enlarge on the different attitudes of the poet and the unnamed man – but he doesn't. Shelley drops from the narrative and instead, it's a moorland walk. A small memory seems important to Browning – the feather and the square of land on which it lies – but everything else, the moorland, its identity, its location, why he was there, all that has vanished. The poem has become a meditation on memory itself, its mysterious gaps, its equally mysterious resonances and connections. As you get older, I find, you're left with more of those tantalising scraps of memory. Now where was that town square, that riverside? What was I doing there? Who was I with? And why did I keep the picture in my head all this time?

Memorabilia   Robert Browning

Ah, did you once see Shelley plain,
　　And did he stop and speak to you,
And did you speak to him again?
　　How strange it seems and new!

But you were living before that,
    And also you are living after;
And the memory I started at –
    My starting moves your laughter.

I crossed a moor, with a name of its own,
    And a certain use in the world no doubt,
Yet a hand's-breadth of it shines alone
    'Mid the blank miles round about:

For there I picked upon the heather
    And there I put inside my breast
A moulted feather, an eagle- feather!
    Well, I forget the rest.

July 8th

I sit rather disconsolately leafing through a huge volume of Kipling poems – just so many of them, and so many *Gor Blimeys* and *'Er Majestys* and *being a man, my son.*

And then that sends me to a copy of *'Puck of Pook's Hill'* and I find my Kipling poem at the start of it – a poem about the layerings of Time and landscape and history. In the Collected Poems, it's given an additional two verses, but I print the *Puck of Pook's Hill* version, which seems to me better.

I never read *Puck of Pook's Hill* as a child, though Richard did, and he says it's one of the books that made him want to be a historian. I would have liked it, I think. I loved *The Jungle Book* and the *Just So Stories*, but Puck never came my way. That started me thinking about books that we didn't read as children – you can read them as an adult, but that's never the same – they can't carve out that place in your life that they would have done if you'd read them when you were young. I never read C.S.Lewis's *Narnia* books. Would I have liked them? I don't like them now – I find them mawkish. But as a child – who knows? I never read *The Lord of the Rings* as a child. I loved it as a young woman, but don't care for it now. My adored reading was mostly historical; Rosemary Sutcliff, Geoffrey Trease. But somehow I missed this one.

Puck's Song   Rudyard Kipling

See you the dimpled track that runs
All hollow through the wheat?
O that was where they hauled the guns
That smote King Philip's fleet.

(Out of the Weald, the secret Weald,
Men sent in ancient years,
The horse –shoes red at Flodden Field,
The arrows at Poitiers!)

See you our little mill that clacks,
So busy by the brook?
She has ground her corn and paid her dues
Ever since Domesday Book.

See you our stilly woods of oak,
And the dread ditch beside?
O that was where the Saxons broke
On the day that Harold died.

See you the windy levels spread
About the gates of Rye?
O that was where the Northmen fled,
When Alfred's ships came by.

See you our pastures wide and lone,
Where the red oxen browse?
O there was a City thronged and known,
Ere London boasted a house.

And see you marks that show and fade,
Like shadows on the Downs?
O they are the lines the Flint Men made,
To guard their wondrous towns.

Trackway and Camp and City lost,
Salt Marsh where now is corn –
Old Wars, old Peace, old Arts that cease,
And so was England born!

She is not any common Earth,
Water or wood or air,
But Merlin's Isle of Gramarye,
Where you and I will fare!

July 9th

Not so long ago, I was complaining of the cold. Now I'm in London on one of the hottest days I remember. Too hot to go into the West End to the exhibition I'd planned to see, so I walk in Shoreditch instead. I want a setting for a story, and Shoreditch seems to be the place.

My first stop is St Leonard's Church – *the bells of Shoreditch*. It's a big empty barn of a church – and there's a pavilion inside . At first I think it's a chapel, but it's full of pictures from girlie magazines, and the word LUST written everywhere. Aha. I spy a Deadly Sin and a themed performance. And then a nice man comes up, and tells me that this is known as the Actor's Church, and shows me the plaque dedicated to all the 16th century actors who worshipped here. It was Shakespeare's parish church at one time, and the Burbages are buried here. Before I go, he shows me some excavations in the grounds and a picture of the old church, the one that Shakespeare would have known.

It's odd that Shakespeare is always associated with Southwark and The Globe – it was to Shoreditch that the young, ambitious, enthusiastic, hardworking Shakespeare came first – it was where he wrote his first plays, presumably had love affairs, and where he lodged.

Last year, I tried, and failed to find the site I'd read about, where Shakespeare's original theatre was being excavated. As I set off from St Leonard's, I found myself in that area again. Before, I'd found a building site off New Inn Road, and assumed that must also be the site of the excavations, but no-one could help me. This year, the building site is now a car park – I wander in, looking for a clue. A young man in a hard hat sees me drifting, and approaches me, asking if I need help. I don't hold out much hope, but today is a day when people are being helpful, so I ask if this is the site of Shakespeare's old theatre. Oh no, he says, you want the dig ; funny, an old man was just asking for it a few minutes ago; it's in New Inn Broadway.

New Inn Broadway, in spite of its grand name, is just a small road, and I'd have missed it, and the excavations. But now I find them, and peer through a fence, and see a small crowd on a viewing platform. A woman comes out, and I ask if the site is accessible. Are you one of our invited guests? she asks. My face falls. No. Oh, she says. Then, But we have another tour starting in ten minutes. Join us if you like.

So I do; a chain of helpful people and coincidences having brought me here.

Also on the site was Holywell Priory, once a fine building with a large chapel, demolished before Burbage started to build his theatre, known simply as The Theatre, and not far from the Curtain theatre. Imagine all the apprentices and smart young blades, swarming out of the Bishopsgate, crowding in the pubs, laughing and yelling, on play days as they made their ways to one or other of these theatres. Respectable folk must have shut their doors firmly.

Shoreditch has always been a scruffy in-between area, on the great road out of London in Roman times, scarcely inhabited after then till the Middle Ages, and in Shakespeare's time, site of all the disreputable places the City Fathers wanted to keep out of London – the Suburb of Sin, the archaeologist calls it. Stow, in his Survey of London, describes an area with a 'continual building of small tenements' as far as the 'ditch' – the old moat - of Shoreditch, which he graphically calls 'sewers ditch'

From the ruins of the priory, the ground slopes down steeply; early theatres were built below ground level in the style of bear pits, and there is a fraction, just a fraction, of the curved outer wall and the groundlings' floor, of Shakespeare's theatre, exposed to sight for the first time maybe since the company did a moonlight flit in 1597. With them, they took the timbers of the demolished buildings, since the owner of the site refused to renew the lease; and rebuilt the theatre across the river in Southwark, that other 'Suburb of Sin.' By that time, Shakespeare was a businessman, and as much a member of the establishment as an actor could ever be. But it was to Shoreditch that the young ardent poet came, on foot, probably, or getting lifts from carters as he could, down through the villages of Uxbridge and Ealing and Shepherd's Bush, along the old Roman road that led alongside the gravelpits of Notting Hill, past the gallows at Tyburn, down the Oxford Road (now Oxford Street), past St Giles, Holborn, Old Street, and the crumbling city walls into the noisy, noisome and fascinating clutter of the City.

Perhaps the Earl of Southampton's mother commissioned the clever and personable young man to write that otherwise strange sequence of sonnets, urging her aristocratic young son to marry – as a Ward of Court, he was under pressure to do this. But the sequence quickly turned into one of the most stunning series of love poems in any language. I've chosen Sonnet 23, with its opening image of stage-fright, something he probably witnessed in this same spot – and maybe even felt himself. Rumours seem to suggest that Shakespeare wasn't perhaps the greatest actor in the troop, specialising in playing old men, or declamatory parts, like the Ghost in Hamlet.

Today, I've been walking in Shakespeare's footsteps, in a location that must have resonated and thrummed with excitement for him

Thank you, nice man in church, man in hard hat, and lady at the excavation. I've had a lovely morning. And I've also found a suitable site for my story. But that, as they say, is another…..

Sonnet XXIII   William Shakespeare

As an unperfect actor on the stage,
Who, with his fear is put besides his part,
Or some fierce thing replete with too much rage,
Whose strength's abundance weakens his own heart;
So I, for fear of trust, forget to say
The perfect ceremony of love's rite,
And in mine own love's strength seem to decay,
O'ercharged with burthen of mine own love's might.
O, let my books be, then, the eloquence

And dumb presagers of my speaking breast;

Who plead for love, and look for recompense,

More than that tongue that more hath more exprest.

O, learn to read what silent love hath writ:

To hear with eyes belongs to love's fine wit.

July 15th

Another from Kipling, another poem about the layerings of landscape, how something of those lost patterns lingers on. Just as I'm sure that something of the spirit of Shakespeare hovers around Shoreditch....

The Way Through the Woods   Rudyard Kipling

They shut the road through the woods

Seventy years ago.

Weather and rain have undone it again,

And now you would never know

There was once a road through the woods

Before they planted the trees.

It is underneath the coppice and heath,

And the thin anemones.

Only the keeper sees

That, where the ring-dove broods,

And the badgers roll at ease,

There was once a road through the woods.

Yet, if you enter the woods

Of a summer evening late,

When the night-air cools on the trout-ringed pools

Where the otter whistles his mate,

(They fear not men in the woods,

Because they see so few)

You will hear the beat of a horse's feet,

And the swish of the skirt in the dew,

Steadily cantering through

The misty solitudes,

As though they perfectly knew

The old lost road through the woods....

But there is no road through the woods.

July !6th

Here's Matthew Arnold, solemn and sober and very nineteenth century. I love the first verse, and the way the poem turns sharply on its hinges at the word 'only' – as the 'grating roar' of the pebbles becomes the 'melancholy' sound of the retreating of the huge sea of Faith. And the magnificent last verse, closing with one of the great lines in English poetry.

Dover Beach   Matthew Arnold

The sea is calm tonight.

The tide is full, the moon lies fair

Upon the straits; - on the French coast the light

Gleams and is gone; the cliffs of England stand,

Glimmering and vast, out in the tranquil bay.

Come to the window, sweet is the night air!

Only, from the long line of spray

Where the sea meets the moon-blanch'd land,
Listen! you hear the grating roar
Of pebbles which the waves draw back and fling,
At their return, up the high strand,
Begin, and cease, and then again begin,
With tremulous cadence slow, and bring
The eternal note of sadness in.

Sophocles long ago
Heard it on the Aegean, and it brought
Into his mind the turbid ebb and flow
Of human misery; we
Find also in the sound a thought,
Hearing it by this distant northern sea.

The Sea of Faith
Was once, too, at the full, and round earth's shore
Lay like the folds of a bright girdle furl'd.
But now I only hear
Its melancholy, long withdrawing roar,
Retreating, to the breath
Of the night-wind, down the vast edges drear
And naked shingles of the world.
Ah, love, let us be true
To one another! For the world, which seems
To lie before us like a land of dreams,
So various, so beautiful, so new,
Hath really neither joy, nor love, nor light,

Nor certitude, nor peace, nor help for pain:
And we are here as on a darkling plain
Swept with confused alarms of struggle and flight,
Where ignorant armies clash by night.

July 29th

I'm staying with the Victorians today, and because he's not a poet for whom modern readers greatly care, I've turned to Tennyson. Like all Victorian poets, there's simply too much of it, and flicking through the collected works is daunting. I'm slightly helped by the fact that my book used to belong to my father (*David Elwyn Thomas, Form 1a Pentre Secondary School* – aaah!) I found it in the family attic when we were clearing things out after my aunt's death. I don't think my father was ever a great poetry reader, though I remember his favourite line was from Milton; Adam addressing Eve; *With thee conversing, I forget all time…*

Still, I'm finding Tennyson hard work. I don't find *In Memoriam* especially moving as a whole; too much of it, too monotonously lachrymose. *Crossing the Bar* is poignant, but it's a funeral poem, and not what I want today.

Instead, I turn to *Ulysses,* a dramatic monologue spoken by the king himself, and my third poem about the wily adventurer. Shakespeare's Ulysses is tricky and clever, Chapman's is struggling against the elements. Tennyson's is austere, aging and restless. He's 'matched with an aged wife' (poor Penelope, after all that tapestry) his people are a 'savage race'. He recalls his travels, and how everything he encountered has changed him irrevocably – my father underlined *I am a part of all that I have met* – and plans to travel again, leaving his son in charge of his kingdom. His mariners are old , but are restless too. The future is uncertain, but it will be heroic.

Tennyson wrote this poem not in his own old age, but in the aftermath of one of his own depressions and the death of his beloved Arthur Hallam. *Though much is taken, much abides...* It's a melancholy poem, with a faint note of stubborn optimism. Much has been written about its point of view, and whether Tennyson is in sympathy with the king, and whether he ought to be; but there seems little point to such speculation; it's an impressive and imaginative recreation of the old king's state of mind. Apparently the Victorians liked the poem more than we do, especially the famous last line.

I learn two things from the web; one is that the carrying over of one line into the first half of the next is called 'enjambment' There's a lot of it in this poem, and it makes for awkward and complex rhythms, in keeping with the difficult and unyielding spirit of the poem. It gives the lie to the idea that Tennyson is a smooth and mellifluous poet; this is one to grapple with, to be confounded and made uneasy by.

The other thing that I learn is that I've always misquoted the famous line I say to myself every summer day as I walk into my garden and see the lavender heads heavy with questing bees. It's *And murmuring of innumerable bees*, and I've never before read the poem from which it's taken, *Come Down O Maid* . And alas, when did I last see an *immemorial elm?*

Ulysses   Alfred, Lord Tennyson

It little profits that an idle king
By this still hearth, among these barren crags,
Matched with an aged wife, I mete and dole
Unequal laws unto a savage race,
That hoard, and sleep , and feed, and know not me.
I cannot rest from travel: I will drink
Life to the lees: all times I have enjoyed
Greatly, have suffered greatly, both with those
That loved me, and alone; on shore, and when
Through scudding drifts the rainy Hyades
Vexed the dim sea: I am become a name
For always roaming with a hungry heart.
Much have I seen and known; cities of men
And manners, climates, councils, governments,
Myself not least, but honoured of them all;
And drunk delight of battle with my peers,
Far on the ringing plains of windy Troy.
I am a part of all that I have met;
Yet all experience is an arch wherethrough
Gleams that untravelled world, whose margin fades
For ever and for ever when I move.
How dull it is to pause, to make an end,
To rust unburnished, not to shine in use!
As though to breathe were life. Life piled on life
Were all too little, and of one to me
Little remains: but every hour is saved
From that eternal silence, something more,

A bringer of new things; and vile it were
For some three suns to store and hoard myself,
And this grey spirit yearning in desire
To follow knowledge like a sinking star
Beyond the utmost bound of human thought.

This my son, mine own Telemachus,
To whom I leave the sceptre and the isle –
Well-loved of me, discerning to fulfil
This labour, by slow prudence to make mild
A rugged people, and through soft degrees
Subdue them to the useful and the good.
Most blameless is he, centred in the sphere
Of common duties, decent not to fail
In offices of tenderness, and pay
Meet adoration to my household gods,
When I am gone. He works his work, I mine.

There lies the port; the vessel puffs her sail:
There gloom the dark broad seas. My mariners,
Souls that have toiled, and wrought, and thought with me-
That ever with a frolic welcome took
The thunder and the sunshine, and opposed
Free hearts, free foreheads – you and I are old;
Old age hath yet his honour and his toil;
Death closes all; but something ere the end,
Some work of noble note, may yet be done,
Not unbecoming men that strove with Gods.

The lights begin to twinkle from the rocks;
The long day wanes: the slow moon climbs: the deep
Moans round with many voices. Come my friends,
'Tis not too late to seek a newer world.
Push off, and sitting well in order smite
The sounding furrows; for my purpose holds
To sail beyond the sunset, and the baths
Of all the western stars , until I die.
It may be that the gulfs will wash us down:
It may be we shall touch the Happy Isles,
And see the great Achilles, whom we knew.
Though much is taken, much abides; and though
We are not now that strength which in old days
Moved earth and heaven: that which we are, we are;
One equal temper of heroic hearts,
Made weak by time and fate, but strong in will
To strive, to seek, to find, and not to yield.

(I thought that the 'baths' of the western stars was a misprint for 'paths', but apparently not. I'm not sure what it means.)

July 31ˢᵗ

I find myself thinking about Philip Sidney's sonnets this morning, and here's one of the most beautiful. Sidney was a courtier, soldier, poet and critic – hard to imagine anyone today being all those things. He died in battle at 32, and at his funeral, thousands lined the route, calling out, according to Fulke Greville, his doting biographer, 'Farewell the worthiest knight that lived, farewell the friend, beloved of all, that hads't no foe but chance.'

We know him best now for his sonnets depicting his unhappy love affair with 'Stella'. Stella was almost certainly Penelope Deveraux, married unhappily at seventeen , to Lord Rich. Sidney seems to suggest that at one point, he missed his chance with Stella and regretted it ever since. Later, he married Frances Walsingham, apparently happily, though he didn't write her any sonnets.

His *Apologie for Poetrie* is written in fluid and alluring prose, with a touch of humour, which makes him sound like someone we'd like to have met: *If you have so earth-creeping a mind that it cannot lift itself up to look to the sky of poetry.... Thus much curse I must send you on behalf of all poets, that while you live, you live in love, and never get favour, for lacking skill of a sonnet; and when you die, your memory die from the earth, for want of an epitaph.*

Astrophel and Stella is one of the most beautiful of Elizabethan sonnet sequences. The poems are full of rhetorical flourish, Cupid, the Muses, Parnassus and a range of gods and goddesses all play their parts, the lover pines, sighs and is generally heartbroken. The address to the Moon in this sonnet is ironical, detached almost. But irresistibly seductive, also, from the sibilant murmurings of the first two lines to the pained declamation of the final couplet. Poor Stella – how could she resist?

Sonnet VI - Astrophel and Stella   Sir Philip Sidney
With how sad steps, O Moon, thou climb'st the skies!
    How silently, and with how wan a face!
  What! May it be that even in heavenly place
That busy archer his sharp arrows tries?

Sure, if that long-with-love-aquainted- eyes
    Can judge of love, thou feel'st a lover's case;
    I read it in thy looks; thy languished grace
To me, that feel the like, thy state descries.
Then, even of fellowship, O Moon, tell me,
    Is constant love deemed there but want of wit?
Are beauties there as proud as here they be?
    Do they above loved to be loved, and yet
    Those lovers scorn whom that love doth possess?
    Do they call virtue there ungratefulness?

August 4th

Philip Sidney led me to his friend Fulke Greville – another poet-aristocrat who published little during his life time. This poem comes from the 'Chorus Sacerdotum' in his tragedy *Mustafa*. Apparently, though this is ostensibly about Suleiman the Magnificent and Turkey, he is really writing about court life under James and Elizabeth. Without the context, it's hard to read this poem properly – but what it says about the conflict between instinct and religion feels surprisingly modern.

The last two lines recall the last line of the first *Astrophel and Stella* sonnet: *Fool, said my Muse to me, Look in thy heart and write.*

From Mustafa   Fulke Greville

Oh wearisome condition of humanity,
Born under one law, to another bound:
Vainly begot, and yet forbidden vanity,
Created sick, commanded to be sound.
What meaneth nature by these diverse laws?
Passion and reason self-division cause.
Is it the mark or majesty of power
To make offences that it may forgive;
Nature herself doth her own self deflower,
To hate those errors she herself doth give.
For how should man think that he may not do
If nature did not fail and punish too?
Tyrant to others, to herself unjust,

Only commands things difficult and hard,

Forbids us all things which it knows is lust,

Makes easy pains, unpossible reward.

If nature did not take delight in blood,

She would have made more easy ways to good.

We that are bound by vows and by promotion,

With pomp of holy sacrifice and rites,

To teach belief in good and still devotion,

To preach of heaven's wonders and delights:

Yet when each of us in his own heart looks

He finds the God there far unlike his books.

August 10th

I'm all alone in the house today, haven't spoken to a soul. Everything quiet except for a buzzard pi-oauing outside in a blue-washed sky. So I take the opportunity to read this poem, one of my favourites, aloud. Not very well, I feel, it's hard to read, the rhythm and the sense of it seeming to tug in different directions. I'm not very good on rhythms, but feel this one is important . I discover it's a 'rare example of a trochaic octameter' – (trochee – stressed followed by unstressed, octameter, eight feet in the line.) It's unusual , anyway.

And there's another hidden rhythm in this poem, a harpsichord recital by the eighteenth century composer Galuppi , unfashionable in Browning's day. We of course can't hear the music, except through the narrator's ears; he feels it is admonitory, critical of the society it describes; underscores the tension between the joyous carnival of Venetian life, and the ubiquity of Death.

And who is the narrator? Not Browning, who may even have written the poem in Venice. The narrator was 'never out of England,' you see him sitting in a book-lined study, but he inhabits an imaginary Venice, - Shylock, Carnival, and the beautiful doomed young people carelessly dancing. Galuppi's reminders of death depress and upset him; the 'cold' music, and the menace of it.

And yet – like most of Browning's poetry, it doesn't quite do what you think it's going to. It's actually a series of narratives buried in each other like a set of Russian dolls; first there's the poet, controlling the whole thing; but you don't hear his voice, or get to know what his own feelings are. Then, there's the fictitious narrator, who was 'never out of England.' Then embedded in his narrative, is Galuppi's voice as the narrator interprets it. Then the 'voices' of the frivolous young people – but this is Galuppi's viewpoint.

The narrator laments the 'dear dead women' – but on his own admission he's never seen them. When I first read this poem, I used to think that the young people were Plague-doomed – but 'Galuppi' has condemned them for frivolity alone. Though his melodies, however 'cold' can't hold all the meaning the narrator imputes to them – as the narrative progresses, you feel it's his own fears he's giving voice to. And he regrets – but what does he regret? And what's he trying to 'reason' that's so overthrown by Galuppi's 'ghostly cricket' music? What's the 'secret' he's trying to squeeze out of nature? He imagines the musician's scorn of the wordly inhabitants of the city, and mourns their loss with one of the most haunting verses in English poetry.

I can do what most of Browning's early readers could never do, and listen to an actual toccata of Galuppi's as I read. It's the Toccata in F major, played evocatively on a harpsichord. I play it again, and read the poem again. It's beautiful music; calm and stately, in my opinion. But it reaches a dramatic surge, just as I read '*Death stepped tacitly and took them where they never see the sun.*'

A Toccata of Galuppi's   Robert Browning.

Oh Galuppi, Baldassaro, this is very sad to find

I can hardly misconceive you; it would prove me deaf and blind:

But although I take your meaning, 'tis with such a heavy mind!

Here you come with your old music, and here's all the good it brings

What, they lived once thus at Venice where the merchants were the kings,

Where St Mark's is, where the Doges used to wed the sea with rings?

Ay, because the sea's the street there; and 'tis arched by…what you call

…Shylock's bridge with houses on it, where they kept the carnival:

I was never out of England – it's as if I saw it all.

Did young people take their pleasure when the sea was warm in May?

Balls and masks begun at midnight, burning ever to mid-day,

Where they made up fresh adventures for the morrow, do you say?

Was a lady such a lady, cheeks so round and lips so red,-

On her neck the small face buoyant, like a bell-flower on its bed,

O'er the breast's superb abundance where a man might base his head?

Well, and it was graceful of them – they'd break talk off and afford

- She to bite her mask's black velvet – he , to finger on his sword,

While you sat and played Toccatas, stately at the clavichord?

What? Those lesser thirds so plaintive, sixths diminished, sigh on sigh,

Told them something? Thos suspensions, those solutions – 'Must we die?'

Those commiserating sevenths – 'Life might last! We can but try!'

'Were you happy?' – 'Yes.' – 'And are you still as happy?' –'Yes. And you?'

-'Then more kisses!' – 'Did *I* stop them, when a million seemed so few?'

Hark, the dominant's persistence till it must be answered to!

So, an octave struck the answer. Oh, they praised you, I dare say!

'Brave Galuppi! that was music! good alike at grave and gay!

'I can always leave off talking when I hear a master play!'

Then they left you for their pleasure: till in due time, one by one,

Some with lives that came to nothing, some with deeds as well undone,

Death stepped tacitly and took them where they never see the sun.

But when I sit down to reason, think to take my stand nor swerve,

While I triumph o'er a secret wrung from nature's close reserve,

In you come with your cold music till I creep thro' every nerve.

Yes, you like a ghostly cricket, creaking where a house was burned:

'Dust and ashes, dead and done with, Venice spent what Venice earned.

'The soul, doubtless, is immortal – where a soul can be discerned.

'Yours, for instance: you know physics, something of geology,

'Mathematics are your pastime; souls shall rise in their degree;

'Butterflies may dread extinction, - you'll not die, it cannot be!

'As for Venice and her people, merely born to bloom and drop,

'Here on earth they bore their fruitage, mirth and folly were the crop:

'What of soul was left, I wonder, when the kissing had to stop?

'Dust and ashes!' So you creak it, and I want the heart to scold.

Dear dead women, with such hair, too – what's become of all the gold

Used to hang and brush their bosoms? I feel chilly and grown old.

August 12th

Last night, the shower of Perseid meteors…

What a beautiful line to write although it's just a news item, almost a poem in itself. I was alone in the house, so around midnight, I opened the bedroom window and looked out. It was an intensely clear night, and full of stars, but not quite dark enough, so the sky seemed to be a kind of mottled charcoal grey rather than black. I shared the space with a single coughing sheep, a distant owl or two and an indignant bat. I couldn't make out the only two constellations I recognise – Orion and the Plough. Instead there seemed to be a blanket of stars; sometimes I couldn't discern background stars from charcoal grey sky, and the more I stared, the more sky and stars seemed to merge in a glimmering dark mesh. Then a great yellow star like a yellow lily climbed higher and higher over the cottage next door– maybe it was Venus.

I was about to give up – I give up easily – when a meteor suddenly splashed across the sky in a broad gold ribbon. I watched for about an hour, during which time I saw perhaps half a dozen others, but never again one as beautiful as the first, threads of silver, arcing, and then gone.

A star poem today by Hopkins

The Starlit Night   Gerard Manley Hopkins

    Look at the stars! look , look up at the skies!
O look at all the fire-folk sitting in the air!
The bright boroughs, the circle-citadels there!
    Down in dim woods the diamond delves! the elves'eyes!
    The grey lawns cold where gold, where quickgold lies!
Wind-beat whitebeam! airy abeles set on a flare!
Flake-doves sent floating forth at a farmyard scare! –
    Ah well! it is all a purchase, all is a prize.
    Buy then! bid then! – What? Prayer, patience, alms, vows.
    Look, look: a May-ness, like on orchard boughts!
Look! March-bloom, like on mealed-with-yellow sallows!
    These are indeed the barn, withindoors house
    The shocks. This piece-bright paling shuts the spouse
Christ home, Christ and his mother and all his hallows.

August 13th

With Richard away at a singing workshop all week, I've been thinking about choirs and music. Hardy of course played the violin in church in his youth as did his father . This poem is perhaps a memory of a story he heard.

We were on holiday in Dorset last year, staying in Lower Brockhampton, next to Hardy's village, and one evening, walked across fields and by a river to his church. No quiet country lanes in Dorset any more, though; mad impatient drivers hurtled by, and we had to shrink into hedgerows to avoid them.

It's a moving poem, this, the contrast of the quiet humility of the choirmaster ; 'if it would not task us,' and the chill practicality of the vicar who overrides his wishes. It's been set to music by Benjamin Britten

The Choirmaster's Burial   Thomas Hardy

He often would ask us
That, when he died,
After playing so many
To their last rest,
If out of us any
Should here abide,
And it would not task us,
We would with our lutes
Play over him
By his grave-brim
The psalm he liked best –
The one whose sense suits

'Mount Ephraim'-
And perhaps we should seem
To him, in Death's dream,
Like the seraphim.

As soon as I knew
That his spirit was gone
I thought this his due,
And spoke thereupon.
'I think,' said the vicar,
'A read service quicker
Than viols out-of-doors
In these frosts and hoars.
The old fashioned way
Requires a fine day,
And it seems to me
It had better not be.'

Hence, that afternoon,
Though never knew he
That his wish could not be,
To get through it faster
They buried the master
Without any tune.

But 'twas said that, when
At the dead of next night
The vicar looked out,

There struck on his ken
Thronged roundabout
Where the frost was graying
The headstoned grass,
A band all in white
Like the saints in church-glass,
Singing and playing
The ancient stave
By the choirmaster's grave.

Such the tenor man told
When he had grown old.

August 17th

This poem is by Erasmus Darwin, poet, philologist, member of the Lunar Society, much married, and grandfather of Charles. The last of the Perseids are streaking across the sky so we are thinking of stars. This poem is strangely prophetic of modern astronomical theories, black holes and red dwarfs, and the creation of one universe out of the destruction of another. I wonder how much reading his grandfather's works started Charles off on his own quest.

Roll on, Ye Stars   Erasmus Darwin

Roll on, ye Stars! exult in youthful prime,
Mark with bright curves the printless steps of Time;
Near and more near your beamy cars approach,
And lessening orbs on lessening orbs encroach;

Flowers of the sky! ye too to age must yield,
Frail as your silken sisters of the field!
Star after star from Heaven's high arch shall rush,
Suns sink on suns, and systems systems crush,
Headlong, extinct, to one dark centre fall,
And Death, and Night and Chaos mingle all!
- Till o'er the wreck, emerging from the storm
Immortal Nature lifts her changeful form,
Mounts from her funeral pyre on wings of flame,
And soars and shines, another and the same.

August 19th

I was surprised to find that my American friend, Diane D'Amico, who knows more about literature than I ever will, didn't know '*Adlestrop*.' It's a favourite British poem, but maybe we've been mean about sharing it with the world. I suppose there are poems that every American schoolchild knows that Brits have never heard of.

Anyway, *Adlestrop* had to go in my poetry year somewhere, so here it is. I can't introduce it better than by quoting Diane:

It was a new poem for me and now wonderful to have. It reminded me of a day years ago when I was standing on the train platform in a isolated spot in England, waiting for the train. I found myself looking at what I suppose were wild tall grasses dotted with waving small red poppies. It wasn't an experience of sound--I don't recall birds--but more an experience of a quiet beauty and stillness, despite the waving of the poppies.

Adlestrop   **Edward Thomas**

Yes, I remember Adlestrop –
The name, because one afternoon
Of heat the express-train drew up there
Unwontedly. It was late June.

The steam hissed. Someone cleared his throat.
No one left and no one came
On the bare platform. What I saw
Was Adlestrop – only the name.

And willows, willow-herb and grass,
And meadow-sweet, and haycocks dry,
No whit less still and lonely fair
Than the high cloudlets in the sky.

And for that minute, a blackbird sang
Close by, and round him, mistier,
Farther and farther, all the birds
Of Oxfordshire and Gloucestershire.

August 22nd

I've been dusting down my Christina Rossetti notes for a talk I have to give soon to our local U3A. I've chosen one of her deceptively simple lyrics – a lament for a love that she has not yet found. Christina seemed to have had two loves in her life – the first, for the timid Pre-Raphaelite James Collinson, who left her to become a Catholic priest (though he never did, in the end) and who, according to her brother, blighted her life for many years; and secondly for an absent-minded but warm-hearted scholar Charles Cayley. She became very close to him about a year or so after writing this poem – but they never married either; I think that she was dissuaded from doing so by one of the over-enthusiastic High Anglican vicars who dominated her life, because Cayley was an agnostic and they deemed it dangerous for her to marry him.

This is a poem seeking companionship as much as love – a voice, a heart, who will share her feelings, maybe in heaven and unfindable, but maybe more simply on earth. Her language is clear and pure – uncluttered, nothing superfluous, no archaisms or consciously 'poetic ' diction, with a perfect grasp of music and rhythm – notice the typically heart-stopping caesura in the third line of the first verse.

Somewhere or Other   Christina Rossetti

Somewhere or other there must surely be
The face not seen, the voice not heard,
The heart that not yet –never yet –ah me!
Made answer to my word.

Somewhere or other, may be near or far:
Past land and sea, clean out of sight:
Beyond the wandering moon, beyond the star
That tracks her night by night.

Somewhere or other, may be far or near:
With just a wall, a hedge between:
With just the last leaves of the dying year
Fallen on a turf grown green.

August 28th

We've been in London for a week, looking after our granddaughter, so there's been very little time for poetry , or anything else, really. Instead, we've been seeing life through a microscope, through the eyes of a two-and-a-half year old. Conversations are intense, focussed, repetitive. Small things – a pigeon on grass, a wet leaf, a man fishing by the canal – cause huge excitements and long discussions; an understanding of life and a personality are slowly being pieced together. It's exciting to be a child growing up in Central London, though Wordsworth wouldn't have agreed.

Reading through my own children's old and much-scribbled-on edition of *The Oxford Book of Poetry for Children* edited by Edward

Blishen, I come across this, almost as short and slight as it's possible for a poem to be; and yet it stays in the mind. In his thoughtful introduction to the anthology, Blishen says, ' Four Ducks 'makes me feel deeply sad; I can't say exactly why.' Just a single line tips it from near-banality to wistful melancholy.

Allingham, an Anglo-Irish poet, is best known for the spooky *The Fairies*, also deceptively simple (*Up the airy mountain, Down the rushy glen, We dare not go a-hunting/ For fear of little men...)* He was a loyal friend of the troubled Dante Gabriel Rossetti.

Four Ducks on a Pond   William Allingham

Four ducks on a pond,
A grass-bank beyond,
A blue sky of spring,
White clouds on the wing;
What a little thing
To remember for years-
To remember with tears!

September

September 1ˢᵗ

Definitely autumn today – though it's been evident for some time now, with a chill in the air, and a crystalline light on the hill. Apples are heavy (too heavy – we should have thinned them) and deep red, and we rescued the plums, just enough for two crumbles, from a bunch of noisy wasps. And the colours in the garden are purple, tawny , flame. I don't plan my garden colours – at least I try to, but something – slugs, a cold winter, a careless bit of digging up-subverts my plans; whatever happened to those lovely deep red daisies I planted the other year? But then, some plants self seed, the toughies survive, and in the end the effect is probably better than if I'd organised it.

One favourite poem is Emily Dickinson's:

> The name-of it – is 'Autumn –
> The hue –of it – is Blood…..

With its whirling movement, its dazzling colours. I love her eddying rose on its vermillion wheels. And there's Keats, of course, and John Clare.

But I discovered this serene and evocative poem by Rainer Maria Rilke the other day, and though my school German is barely good enough to be able to limp through it with a dictionary, I think it must have a part in my poetry year. Professor Mary Kinzie has kindly allowed me to use her lovely translation. The transition from the imagery in the first seven lines of plenitude and richness to the mood of resigned solitude in the last five is disconcerting, yet also strangely calming .

Herbsttag   Rainer Maria Rilke

Herr; es ist Zeit. Der Sommer war sehr gross.
Leg deinen Schatten auf die Sonnenuhren,
und auf den Fluren lass the Winde los.

Befiel den letzen Früchten voll zu sein:
gib ihnen noch zwei südlichere Tage,
dränge sie zur Vollendung hin und jage
die letze Süsse in den schweren Wein.

Wer jetzt kein Haus hat, baut sich keines mehr.
Wer jetz allein ist, wird es lange bleiben,
wird wachen, lessen, lange Briefe schreiben
und wird in den Alleen hin und her
unruhig wandern, wenn die Blätter treiben.

Day in Autumn - *trans* Mary Kinzie

After the summer's yield, Lord, it is time
to let your shadow lengthen on the sundials
and in the pastures let the rough winds fly.

As for the final fruits, coax them to roundness.
Direct on them two days of warmer light
to hale them golden toward their term, and harry
the last few drops of sweetness through the wine.

Whoever's homeless now, will build no shelter;
who lives alone will live indefinitely so,
waking up to read a little, draft long letters,
and, along the city's avenues,
fitfully wander, when the wild leaves loosen.

September 3ʳᵈ

Instead of a day of mists and mellow fruitfulness in Wales; I'm going up the Holloway Road to see my daughter, who has got herself a broken foot (dancing at a wedding – a better way to go than slithering on wet leaves as happened to me a few years ago) Lucy lives in a quiet street off the road; but Holloway Road has resisted all attempts at gentrification, and remains unapologetically and unashamedly itself. There's The Titanic Café, Samson Barber's Shop, Miss Desire, the Salon des Artistes Men's Hairdressers, the Blood Brothers Tattoo Parlour, The Gunners Spice Indian restaurant , at least three Paradise Cafes - and impressively, and unexpectedly, a Daniel Libeskind building. Cafes with bright red and yellow fascias show laminated pictures of burgers the size of large rocks. Arsenal's glittering new Emirates stadium rises like a glass cathedral in the distance

And yet , though it's hotly in denial of a past, the road has its own deep history. Once, a wide, muddy track, an ancient 'hollow way,' taking a gentle hilly curve through fields away from London and to the North, it's been monastic land, an execution site, and a place for medieval archers to practice, though its most famous resident is probably the fictional Pooter. Dick Whittington and his cat have a monumental stone at the northern end, the spot where he 'turned again'

Another resident, living in a long gone house, off Bowman's Place (where the archers once assembled) was Edward Lear, and I'm reminded of him because my daughter's choice of a poem is *The Owl and the Pussycat*, which I used to read to her years ago.

Lear was the youngest of twenty-one children and by the time she got round to having him, his mother seems to have tired of the whole business, and he was largely brought up by his much older sister Ann. They had to leave what was then a fine house with country views, when his father briefly spent time in a debtor's prison. Later the parents bought a small house with room for only a couple of children; and Edward and Ann set up home together. He became an artist and a traveller. It's been assumed that he was homosexual, though some biographers deny this. At any rate, though he was a sociable man, at heart he was lonely and melancholy - and this melancholy comes through even in his comic verse.

I find this poem, The Owl and the Pussycat, strangely sad. Maybe it's the odd love between the incompatible creatures ('*Begotten by despair/ Upon impossibility*' always comes to mind) that long long voyage and the lonely moonlight celebration at the end of it. And apparently, something about it unnerves my granddaughter too.

The Owl and The Pussycat   Edward Lear

i

The Owl and the Pussy-cat went to sea
In a beautiful pea-green boat,
They took some honey, and plenty of money,
Wrapped up in a five-pound note.
The Owl looked up to the stars above,
And sang to a small guitar,
'O lovely Pussy! O Pussy my love,
What a beautiful Pussy you are,
You are,
You are!
What a beautiful Pussy you are!'

ii

Pussy said to the Owl, 'You elegant fowl!
How charmingly sweet you sing!
O let us be married! Too long we have tarried:
But what shall we do for a ring?'
They sailed away, for a year and a day,
To the land where the Bong-tree grows
And there in a wood, a Piggy-wig stood,
With a ring at the end of his nose,
His nose,
His nose,
With a ring at the end of his nose.

iii

'Dear Pig, are you willing to sell for one shilling
Your ring?' Said the Piggy, 'I will.'
So they took it away, and were married next day
By the Turkey who lives on the hill.
They dined on mince, and slices of quince,
Which they ate with a runcible spoon;
And hand in hand, on the edge of the sand,

They danced by the light of the moon,
   The moon,
   The moon,
They danced by the light of the moon.

September 4th

I'd wanted to take some poetry to London with me; the poet I'd like to read is Byron, but my volume (Nonesuch Edition - clear, good print, creamy paper, good binding) is too heavy, so instead, I take my Milton - Oxford University Press, navy cloth binding, clear print, opens flat, thinnest India paper. Can you buy either of these editions now, I wonder?

I call it 'my' Milton, but it actually isn't. I brought it from a second hand bookshop - in Streatham, I think, for half-a-crown many years ago. Before then it belonged to Kenneth S Woodroofe, who was at Oxford in 1948. Nearly all the underlinings and annotations are his - he seems to have especially studied Book II. I don't get the impression he loved Milton. And he got rid of this nice edition, which must have been expensive when new. Of course I've just now Googled him, and find that he was an English professor in America and Japan, has written books on religion and Keats.

I like to be the second or third possessor of a poetry book. I like to imagine those other hands turning the pages, those other senses gathering their impressions, those other eyes scanning the lines. It makes each book into a kind of ghost-palimpsest; layers of feelings and thoughts and recollections, each individual's take on each poem slightly different, each remembering in a different way. I've lived with Kenneth S Woodroofe now for so long, he almost feels like a friend.

My copy of Dryden's Poems, (also an Oxford Edition, but the standard one, with slightly thicker paper) belonged to Ursula K Everest, who was at Oxford in 1942. She's even left one of her essays inside: *Thus Dryden, as a satirist, shows himself able, not only to use his verse, with its new clarity and freedom from elaborate imagery, gained through years of dramatic writing…..but …..to vary his satire methods according to the demands of his subject.*

I feel I like Ursula, on no particular evidence. I also, through intensive research (okay, I asked the owner of the second-hand bookshop) found out who she was – a local headmistress , recently died. But what of Lewys T Virgo, whose friends Geoff and Molly gave him a copy of *The Oxford Book of Seventeenth Century Verse* in 1942, bought from Thurnam's bookshop in Carlisle? He's left no trace on the book. And what did C. Bushell think of the copy of Mrs Browning's Poems that Mother and Dad bought for her (I'm guessing her) in June 1917? Horsfield (no initial, so probably a he) took his 1966 *Elizabethan Lyrics* edited by Kenneth Muir with grim seriousness. (*Read Intro. P XXVI. Twice. Read it through. Then go through it again with finger in text.*) Sometimes, the second hand bookshop throws you someone you've heard of. My *Elizabethan Lyrics* edited by Norman Ault (a lovely edition) belonged to Neville Coghill, Chaucer's translator, and my Traherne passed through Mrs W.B.Yeats's hands.

I remember my father's Milton quote, so I look it up. (Kenneth also thought it worth underlining in ink.) I'm a bit disappointed to find it's subservient Eve who's speaking, not Adam, as I thought. I'll leave out the subservient bits.

From   Paradise Lost Book IV   John Milton

With thee conversing I forget all time,
All seasons and thir change, all please alike.
Sweet is the breath of morn, her rising sweet,
With charm of earliest Birds; pleasant the Sun
When first on this delightful land he spreads
His orient Beams, on herb, tree, fruit, and flour,
Glistring with dew; fragrant the fertile earth
After soft showers; and sweet the coming on
Of grateful Eevning milde, then silent Night

With this her solemn Bird and this fair Moon
And these the Gemms of Heav'n, her starrie train:
But neither breath of Morn when she ascends
With charm of earliest Birds, nor rising Sun
On this delightful land, nor herb, fruit, floure,
Glistring with dew, nor fragrance after showers,
Nor grateful Evening mild, not silent Night
With this her solemn Bird, nor walk by Moon,
Or glittering Starr-light without thee is sweet.

September 7th

London is paralysed by a Tube strike ; last time I looked, the New
North Road was clogged up with snail's pace traffic. I need to go
out later on, but I can walk, so until then, why not sit at home
reading Milton? Coincidentally, the *Guardian*'s Poem of the Week -
which triggered off my Poetry Year - is Milton's *Lycidas*, so he
seems to be in the air today. At school, we 'did' *Samson Agonistes* - I
remember moving from dislike - it's very easy to dislike the priggish
bits of Milton and the misogyny - to awe and admiration. I
remember being entranced by

> *Sabrina fair,*
>> *Listen where thou art sitting*
> *Under the glassie, cool, translucent wave*
>> *In twisted braids of Lilies knitting*
> *The loose train of thy amber-dropping hair*

saying it to myself over and over, listening to the way the
consonants plait themselves together.

Thick as Autumnal Leaves that strow the Brooks
In Vallombrosa, where th'Etrurian shades
High overarch't imbower….

Here are the surprisingly gentle last lines of *Paradise Lost,* reflecting a Protestant optimism rather than Catholic gloom. It makes a contrast with Massacio's terrible image of the expulsion from Eden, in which Adam and Eve convulsed by fear and grief, vainly try to cover their suddenly shameful nakedness.

From Paradise Lost Book XII   John Milton

……now too nigh
Th'Archangel stood, and from the other Hill
To thir fixt Station, all in bright array
The Cherubim descended: on the ground
Gliding meteorous, as Ev'ning Mist
Ris'n from a River o're the marish glides,
And gathers ground fast at the Labourers heel
Homeward returning. High in Front advanc't,
The brandisht Sword of God before them blaz'd
Fierce as a Comet: which with torrid heat,
And vapour as the Libyan Air adust,
Began to parch that temperate Clime: whereat
In either hand the hastning Angel caught
Our lingring Parents, and to th' Eastern Gate
Led them direct, and down the Cliff as fast
To the subjected Plaine; then disappeer'd.
They looking back, all th' Eastern side beheld

Of Paradise, so late thir happie seat,
Wav'd over by that flaming Brand, the gate
With dreadful Faces throng'd and fierie Armes:
Some natural tears they drop'd, but wip'd them soon;
The World was all before them, where to choose
Thir place of rest, and Providence thir guide:
They hand in hand with wandring steps and slow ,
Through *Eden* took thir solitarie way.

September 15th

A few days in Wales before it's back to Hoxton and the Holloway Road. We have a friend staying with us, and we go to Brecon Cathedral. A strange cathedral, this, tucked into the folds and winds of this hilly little town, it effectively hides itself , until you suddenly come across it in its snug close, surrounded by trees, whose leaves are just now starting to turn. There's no grand entrance, just a funny little side door which looks as though it leads into a kitchen, a dull hallway, and then the cathedral interior opens out, austere, calm and beautiful. We look at military flags and the great marble memorials that the nineteenth century loved, swooning maidens and drooping laurels in chilly white, and the slate floor tombs of the seventeenth century, with their blocky writing going round in intricate mazes and patterns, all those Edwards and Margarets and Lewises and Watkyns. Some beautiful early monuments that escaped Cromwell – many didn't of course. And a font with the weird and wild stylized leaves and peering faces of the Herefordshire school.

We go on to Tretower, the calm grey fortified manor house on the Usk, some of its empty rooms recently restored. In the seventeenth century it was owned by the Vaughan family, an uncle of Henry and Thomas, and the two boys must have visited.

An excuse for another poem by The Silurist. Wordsworth didn't have the monopoly on childhood, though Vaughan's awareness of innocence is contrasted more dogmatically with Sin than Wordsworth's was. *Bright shoots of everlastingnesse* – lovely.

The Retreate   Henry Vaughan

Happy those early dayes! when I
Shin'd in my Angell-infancy.
Before I understood this place
Appointed for my second race,
Or taught my soul to fancy ought
But a white, Celestiall thought,
When yet I had not walkt above
A mile, or two, from my first love,
And looking back (at that short space,)
Could see a glimpse of his bright-face:
When on some gilded Cloud, or flower
My gazing soul would dwell an houre,
And in those weaker glories spy
Some shadows of eternity:
Before I taught my tongue to wound
My Conscience with a sinfull sound,
Or had the black art to dispence
A sev'rall sinne to ev'ry sence,

But felt through all this fleshly dresse
Bright shoots of everlastingnesse.
O how I long to travel back
And tread again that ancient track!
That I might once more reach that plaine,
Where first I left my glorious traine,
From whence th'Inlightned spirit sees
That shady City of Palme trees:
But (ah!) my soul with too much stay
Is drunk, and staggers in the way.
Some men a forward motion love,
But I by backward steps would move,
And when this dust falls to the urn
In that state I came return.

September 20th

Another train journey to London and the book I havetohaveto read is Jane Eyre. I don't know why these compulsions to read a particular book arise – in this case it was seeing a few lines quoted in a newspaper article. It's a book I've read many times , but now probably not for ten years or so. Each time it's a slightly different book, just as I am a slightly different reader. I've long ago left the days where Rochester was my romantic hero. A garrulous, bad tempered bigamist? Thank you, but no thank you. But I'm still gripped by the story.

'There was no possibility of taking a walk that day…' The first time I read these words was probably on just such a dreary day - a wintery Saturday afternoon, curled in one of my parents' big armchairs, a

coal fire glowing, rain beating against the windows. I'd riffle through their bookshelves looking for books that attracted me. Usually I just read the first chapters, if I was fortunate enough to find a book in which a childhood was described. And that description of Jane's nightmare day at her aunt's, and her journey to Lowood absorbed me. It wasn't till I was fourteen or so that I wanted to venture beyond Lowood and meet the story's hero.

The copy I'm reading now is the one I had as a girl: *Frances Ann Thomas* written inside in rather ugly backward sloping handwriting. A Collins Edition, bound in red artificial leather, thin paper, quite small print. It's become detached from its cover now, and bears the yellow scars of several old sellotape mendings, so probably it's time I got a new copy. That's the nice things about books - any edition, a cheap Penguin classic, the scribbled on one that my daughter had at school, would give the same pleasure. We knew someone once who had a first edition. I was dying to handle it - but I wasn't allowed anywhere near. Literally. The owner stood across the room, gingerly holding out the small unremarkable volume in its ostentatious slip case. But no-one was ever going to *read* that particular book again.

I notice that I've made some marks in my much-handled and everyday edition. For the life of me I can't see why I underlined some of the things I did. I don't habitually mark my books unless I'm studying them, and Jane Eyre escaped the dead hand of a syllabus on her shoulder. Looking at those marks makes young Frances Ann Thomas almost as unknown a quantity as Kenneth or Ursula.

You can't help imagining Charlotte scribbling away in a hotel while her father was recovering from gruesome cataract surgery. Eyes and seeing must have been much on her mind - though that doesn't explain why she feels it necessary to blind her hero at the end. Shutting him up might have been a better idea.

But this journal is about poetry, not novels. Charlotte Bronte did write poetry, but the frigid rhetoric which can mar her prose hangs heavier in her poetry. Her sister Emily wrote a handful of masterpieces, this among them.

No Coward Soul is Mine   Emily Bronte

No Coward Soul is mine
No trembler in the world's storm-troubled sphere,
I see Heaven's glories shine
And Faith shines equal arming me from Fear.

O God within my breast
Almighty ever-present Deity,
Life – that in me has rest,
As I Undying Life, have power in Thee.

Vain are the thousand creeds
That move men's hearts, unutterably vain,
Worthless as withered weeds
Or idlest froth amid the boundless main,

To waken doubt in one
Holding so fast by thy infinity
So surely anchored on
The steadfast rock of Immortality.

With wide-embracing love
Thy spirit animates eternal years
Pervades and broods above,
Changes, sustains, dissolves, creates and rears.

Though earth and man were gone,
And suns and universes ceased to be
And Thou wert left alone
Every existence would exist in thee.

There is not room for Death
Nor atom that his might could render void,
Thou – THOU art Being and Breath,
And what THOU art may never be destroyed.

September 22nd

By bus to the South Bank, and London at its best, pale blues and soft greys with jewel touches of scarlet; the river brimming, and white bridges arching like wings all in clear autumn sunshine. The riverside used to be our private walk, but now it's become fashionable and full of the usual array of fire-eaters and silver statues, sweating runners, cyclists, loud mobile-phoners .But I don't mind - I like everyone to be celebrating London.

I'd hoped to walk from the Festival Hall to the Millennium Bridge to pay my respects to Dr Donne in St Paul's, but building works threw me up to the surface at Blackfriars, so I walked to Fleet Street, past the ghost of the terrace where Dante Gabriel once lived with Lizzie Siddall, following the course of the Fleet River, past what was once a holy well, and then became Bridewell prison, up to the street where the presses no longer rumble away and the journalists no longer hang out.

Wordsworth was crossing London on just such a silvery September morning, before fires were lit, and before the rumble of cartwheels started up over the cobbles. He and his sister Dorothy were on their way to France, to meet his daughter for the first time. He was about to get married to a woman who wasn't the mother of that child, and it was set to be an emotional meeting. I imagine him sitting erect and silent among huddled early morning passengers by the window, gazing sternly out, Dorothy watching him like a hawk, but not daring to break the poetic reverie with words. But that evening, she wrote about the event in her diary; '*It was a beautiful morning. The city, St Paul's, with the river, and a multitude of little boats made a most beautiful sight as we crossed Westminster Bridge. The houses were not overhung by their cloud of smoke and they were spread out endlessly, yet the sun shone so brightly, with such a fierce light, that there was something like the purity of one of nature's own grand spectacles.*' Maybe it was after looking at her words, that Wordsworth was inspired, as so often he was, to transform the prose into poetry. She was, as he acknowledged, his 'eyes and ears.'

Upon Westminster Bridge   William Wordsworth

Earth has not anything to show more fair:
Dull would he be of soul who could pass by
A sight so touching in its majesty:
The City now doth like a garment wear

The beauty of the morning: silent , bare,
Ships, towers, domes, theatres and temples lie
Open unto the fields and to the sky,
All bright and glittering in the smokeless air.

Never did sun more beautifully steep
In his first splendour valley, rock or hill;
Ne'er saw I , never felt, a calm so deep!
The river glideth at his own sweet will:
Dear God! The very houses seem asleep;
And all that mighty heart is lying still!

September 26th

A cold, colourless day in London, and I hear that it's the same in Wales. And a heavy frost last night, so that's my nasturtiums done for. What with spending these unexpected weeks in London and going away on holiday next week, my garden is going to get entirely neglected this autumn; will have to wait for spring for its clear-up. Most of me is disappointed by this, but a small and subversive voice is whispering *Go on, you're relieved, really; you know you are!*

Anyway, relieved or not, there's to be no digging, no pruning, no building of bonfires or sweeping of leaves, no heaping up of dead lavender, or untangling of scented brambles, no shaking of seed-heads, or ripping up the invasive silvery dead-nettle. So I shall have to let a poem do all that for me instead; here's Edward Thomas.

Digging   Edward Thomas

To-day I think
Only with scents, - scents dead leaves yield,
And bracken, and wild carrot's seed,
And the square mustard field;
Odours that rise
When the spade wounds the root of tree,
Rose, currant, raspberry, or goutweed,
Rhubarb or celery;
The smoke's smell, too,
Flowing from where a bonfire burns
The dead, the waste, the dangerous,
And all to sweetness turns.
It is enough
To smell, to crumble the dark earth,
While the robin sings over again
Sad songs of Autumn mirth.

September 27th

We're starting to prepare for our holiday in Greece next week, and brushing up on Greek mythology. I was looking out of our flat, wondering about today's poem, when a swan glided elegantly past, through the sludge coloured waters of the Regents Canal; there was my poem; Greek mythology plus swan.

The most famous Leda and the Swan poem is the heart-stopping one by Yeats. But I like this shorter one too, by D.H. Lawrence. I love the way the soft sibilance of the first two lines changes to a dramatic hiss in the fourth; and then the sensual squelchiness of the last two lines; you can almost smell the water and the mud.

My father used to teach at the school in Norwood where Lawrence had taught many years earlier. There was little trace of him left, except for one elderly teacher, who claimed to have been the original of Miriam in *Sons and Lovers*. And there was a caretaker who'd been there in Lawrence's day. My father asked if he remembered him. The caretaker scratched his head and said, 'Lawrence? Oh yes, Mr Lawrence. Bit of a painter wasn't he? Don't think he was much of a teacher, though.'

Leda   D.H. Lawrence

Come not with kisses
not with caresses
of hands and lips and murmurings;
come with a hiss of wings
and sea-touch tip of a beak
and treading of wet, webbed, wave-working feet
into the marsh-soft belly

September 28th

Of course I *know* Greece; I've travelled with Odysseus, tasting the salty wind on my sun-cracked face, hidden behind rocks and laughed as the crazed Polyphemus howls 'No-body blinded me! No-body!'. I've strained and struggled with the young Theseus to lift the stone, and on the day he was finally successful watched the smile of joy on his young face fade as he turned to see his mother's tears. I've wandered with distraught Demeter, through windswept cornfields. I know the white temples, the piny hills, the anenome-starred slopes. I've watched the Greek fleet setting off for Troy, met Oedipus at a dusty crossroad, I'd know what to do if I suddenly encountered Medusa.

But the thing is, I've never actually *been* there. I must be almost the last person in Britain who can say that they've never been to this most commonplace of holiday destinations. And I'm a little anxious. For everyone keeps a picture of an unvisited place in their heads, to be suddenly replaced by the real thing the minute you step out of the plane or the car. Your imaginary place is lost, never to return.

Sometimes, the real thing is far more beautiful - both India and Italy far surpassed their imaginary equivalents. Egypt, of which I'd seen so many pictures, was spookily similar but not quite the same. New York, which had existed in a kind of velvety black-and-white, was romantic but much grubbier. And sometimes, places disappoint; you lose your imaginary city to no benefit.

My imaginary Greece, I know, is partly a Victorian construct, those pure white temples, those chaste marbles, those graceful and gliding men and women, those glittering heroes and gods. That wine-dark sea…. Too much exposure to the pictures in *The Children's Encyclopedia* in my childhood there. Ancient Greece was a brash and noisy and garish place, no doubt; and as for those women, they might have been lovely, but you wouldn't have caught a glimpse of them. I know Greece will be beautiful; but I shall miss my Greece-in-the-head when it's lost.

Keats never went to Greece, but he wrote one of the greatest poems about a place unvisited, a culture imagined, melodies unheard….

Ode on a Grecian Urn   John Keats

Thou still unravished bride of quietness!
    Thou foster-child of Silence and slow Time,
Sylvan historian, who canst thus express
    A flowery tale more sweetly than our rhyme:
What leaf-fringed legend haunts about thy shape
    Of deities or mortals, or of both,
      In Tempe or the vales of Arcady?
 What men and gods are these? What maidens loth?
What mad pursuit? What struggle to escape?
    What pipes and timbrels? What wild ecstacy?

Heard melodies are sweet, but those unheard
    Are sweeter: therefore, ye soft pipes, play on;
Not to the sensual ear, but, more endear'd,
    Pipe to the spirit ditties of no tone:
Fair youth, beneath the trees, thou canst not leave
    Thy song, nor ever can those trees be bare:
    Bold lover, never never canst thou kiss,
Though winning near the goal- yet, do not grieve;
    She cannot fade, though thou hast not thy bliss,
For ever wilt thou love and she be fair!

Ah, happy happy boughs! That cannot shed
    Your leaves, nor ever bid the Spring adieu;
And happy melodies, unwearied,
    For ever piping songs for ever new;
More happy love! more happy, happy love!

For ever warm and still to be enjoy'd,
    Forever panting and forever young;
All breathing human passion far above,
    That leaves a heart high sorrowful and cloy'd,
    A burning forehead, and a parching tongue.

Who are these coming to the sacrifice?
    To what green altar, O mysterious priest,
Lead'st thou that heifer lowing at the skies,
    And all her silken flanks with garlands drest?
What little town by river or sea-shore,
    Or mountain-built with peaceful citadel,
    Is emptied of its folk, this pious morn?
And little town, thy streets for evermore
    Will silent be; and not a soul to tell
    Why thou are desolate, can e'er return.

O attic shape! Fair attitude! with brede
    Of marble men and maidens overwrought,
With forest branches, and the trodden weed;
    Thou, silent form, dost tease us out of thought
As doth eternity: Cold Pastoral!
    When old age shall this generation waste,
    Thou shalt remain, in midst of other woe
    Than ours, a friend to man, to whom thou say'st,
'Beauty is truth, truth beauty, - that is all
    Ye know on earth, and all ye need to know.'

September 29th

I seem to have stood at an awful lot of bus stops in the rain, and got on an awful lot of red buses recently. But I am a person-going-to-Greece, and rather than writing about any of this humdrum stuff, I shall bring in Lord Byron, who unlike Keats, did get to Greece, though it didn't do him, or Greece, much good in the end.

Strangely, this poem, which usually stands alone, is actually tucked away in the irony-ridden pages of *Don Juan* where it is given to a cynical poet who will sing, with minimal sincerity, verses appropriate to whichever nation he finds himself among.

From The Isles of Greece   Lord Byron

The Isles of Greece, the Isles of Greece!
    Where burning Sappho loved and sung,
Where grew the arts of War and Peace,
    Where Delos rose and Phoebus sprung!
Eternal summer gilds them yet,
But all, except their Sun, is set,

The Scian and the Teian muse,
    The Hero's harp, the Lover's lute,
Have found the fame your shores refuse:
    Their place of birth alone is mute
To sounds which echo further west
Than your Sires' 'Islands of the Blest,'

The mountains look on Marathon –
    And Marathon looks on the sea;

And musing there an hour alone,
    I dreamed that Greece might still be free;
For standing on the Persians' grave,
I could not deem myself a slave.

October

October 1st

In more pouring rain, to the British Museum, for some Greek homework. I have the first galleries pretty much to myself, so I'm able to learn how to tell my black-figure from my red-figure, my archaic from my classical, my Doric from my Ionic. I'm also wondering about Keats' Urn (in between trying to banish Richard's awful joke which has got itself like an earworm into my consciousness -*What's a Grecian Urn? About fifty drachma a week. SHUDDUP, willya?)*

The first time I actually looked at Greek vases - rather than hurrying past them - was in Sicily, where I saw how fascinating and subtle they could be. So I enjoy looking at them today, even though many of the Greek galleries are inconveniently closed. Then it's into the maelstrom of the Elgin Marbles, battling through stentorian German tour guides, Japanese taking photos of themselves, art students making bad drawings. I can 't get really close to the marbles, but suddenly that's an advantage. Normally, I'm a peerer - I like to get up close and squint; but today I have to stand back, and for the first time am really aware of the wonderful movement of the North Frieze, all those horses, jostling and rearing, that amazing jumble of legs, that surging, swirling, confusing advance.

On the South Frieze, there's 'the heifer lowing at the skies' which is supposed to have inspired Keats. He came with Haydon one day to see the marbles, and sat before them transfixed for a couple of hours. When I imagine the Grecian Urn in the poem, what I see isn't black-or-red figure terracotta, but something white, or even blue-and-white Wedgewood. But maybe that isn't so silly; the Grecian urn is an idealised one, a composite. The Elgin marbles contributed, and in the Keats-Shelley house in Rome there's a tracing, made by Keats, of the Sosibos vase in Paris. This is a graceful narrow urn, 'leaf-fringed' around the neck, with a sequence of still, calm self-contained figures in slow movement around it. And it's white marble, so maybe so was Keats' idealised urn.

I leave the British Museum, journey back on two buses, with a rain- drenched walk between them, past an anti-vivisection demonstration, Roman wall fragments, Postman's Park, Wood Street, ('*On the corner of Wood Street, when daylight appears, hangs a thrush who sings loud; it has sung for two years...*') and then round to catch my last bus by Moorgate and Finsbury Pavement, where the young Keats lived before the series of tragedies that tore him and his family apart for ever. The start and end of my journey both link to Keats, so I must choose Keats again, even though it's the second time this week. This is the sonnet he wrote after being transfixed by the Elgin marbles.

Unlike the *Grecian Urn*, there's nothing here descriptive of what he saw; all that went into deep consciousness; instead he writes of his mood, half dreaming, half despairing. It's the state he described as 'negative capability' - that poetic capacity to absorb greedily, while apparently in a state of mental suspension; 'when a man is capable of being in uncertainties, Mysteries, doubts, without any irritable reaching after fact and reason.'

It's a curious sonnet, though; none of the confident euphoria of *On First Looking into Chapman's Homer*. A couple of months earlier, he and Leigh Hunt had crowned each other with ivy and laurel. Some ladies arrived on an unexpected visit; Hunt snatched his crown off, but Keats, half proud, half embarrassed, kept his on and wrote a sonnet about the incident: *To The Ladies Who Saw Me Crown'd*. It was a trivial incident, but an important one for Keats – he was standing up and saying to the world, 'Look, I am a poet. Laugh if you dare.' Now, he has taken his newly defined poetic self to view the wonders of antiquity; he's awed and confused and daunted by their grandeur and beauty; they have survived, but they fill him full of thoughts of death. But also – only half glimpsed – something beyond death.

On First Seeing The Elgin Marbles   John Keats

My spirit is too weak: mortality
Weighs heavily on me like unwilling sleep,
And each imagined pinnacle and steep
Of godlike hardship tells me I must die
Like a sick eagle looking at the sky.
Yet 'tis a gentle luxury to weep
That I have not the cloudy winds to keep
Fresh for the opening of the morning's eye.
Such dim-conceived glories of the brain
Bring round the heart an indescribable feud;
So do these wonders a most dizzy pain,
That mingles Grecian grandeur with the rude
Wasting of old Time – with a billowy main,
A sun, a shadow of a magnitude.

October 11th

The distant hills are lost in a violet haze of mist, the sea is ruffled, and the rain pours down, making swirling brown floods in the gutters. I huddle beneath my raincoat. No, this isn't Wales, but Nauplion in the Peloponnese. But yesterday, we went to Tiryns and Mycenae, I walked through the Lion Gate and 'gazed upon the face of Agamemnon' – the golden death mask that Schliemann found. Only of course it wasn't that – the real thing's in Athens, and the mask in the museum is a copy. And it wasn't Agamemnon anyway, but a king who lived four centuries earlier.

We stumbled up rocky slopes scattered with wild cyclamen, and tried to read the palaces and places of Homer into stony lines of foundations. In the museum, we saw modern reconstructions of the faces of some of those buried kings and queens; they were surprisingly homely – in the English sense of the word – with high cheekbones, wide set eyes and noses flattened at the bridge. They looked like a family, but they were a family without names and stories. Strange that though so sophisticated, though they scattered exquisite gold filigree over the dead, made finely chased weapons, and painted elegant frescoes, these people used their writing to record nothing more interesting than shopping lists, inventories of things.

But we looked into the steeply sloping valley at Agamemnon's view, surprisingly unspoiled, pale bare hills, dotted with olives and thorns.

Today – also in the rain – we go the great ancient theatre at Epidaurus. We learn that the Greek word for 'actor' is *hypocrites* , meaning 'under judgement.' I guess being judged inevitably leads to insincerity. And the word 'tragedy' means 'goatsong' – and nobody knows why.

I wasn't expecting a poem today, but our guide is demonstrating the acoustics of the theatre, Our party , and everyone else's, fall silent as she reads a poem new to me, but now a favourite , Cavafy's *Ithaca*, a meditation on journeys.

> *When you set out on your journey to Ithaca*
> *Pray that the road is long…*

Here's another poem about journeys, and how the journey is often more creative than the arrival. It's the great Walt again, in good swaggering mode. But I like this poem, and its ebullience.

From   Song of the Open Road   Walt Whitman

The earth expanding right hand and left hand,

The picture alive, every part in its best light,

The music falling in where it is wanted, and stopping where it is not wanted,

The cheerful voice of the public road – the gay fresh sentiment of the road.

O highway I travel! O public road! do you say to me, *Do not leave me?*

Do you say, *Venture not? If you leave me, you are lost?*

Do you say, *I am already prepared – I am well beaten and undenied – adhere to me?*

O public road! I say back, I am not afraid to leave you – yet I love you:

You express me better than I can express myself:

You shall be more to me than my poem.

I think heroic deeds were all conceiv'd in the open air, and all great poems also:

I think I could stop here myself, and do miracles;

(My judgements, thoughts, I henceforth try by the open air, the road;)

I think whatever I shall meet on the road I shall like, and whoever beholds me shall like me;

I think whoever I see must be happy.

October 14th

Posiedon has been hurtling torrential rain and thunderbolts at us all night. And we hear of a strike of guards at the Parthenon, which we're supposed to see tomorrow. The site is closed, with riot police everywhere. The guards haven't been paid for ages, so you can't really blame them. But not an auspicious start to our day in Delphi.

The Delphi-in-my-head is situated on a quiet slope, reached through a meandering path under the dappled shade of pine trees, grass scented with narcissus, no sound except the gentle chirrup of finches. The temple is white and quiet, a single priest looking calmly up at us as we approach….

We go to the museum first, hoping the rain will stop, and the Delphi-in-my-head gives a gentle sigh and starts to fade. But we see marvellous frescoes and statues and learn of the real thing.

And then the rain stops and we're off to the Oracle itself. Far from being on any gentle slope or piny grove, we're in a great, steep valley, and the shrine is poised vertiginously on a great fall of hill, steep cliffs rearing up all around, stained with falls of paprika-coloured rock – the 'flames' of Apollo. And the mountain – wondrously – is Mount Parnassus. The Sacred Way snakes up and up the mountainside, and in ancient times would have been cramped and crowded with the citadels of various grateful cities, bristling and glittering with statues and trophies, shoved wherever they could find space.

And then finally the great marble temple, sacrifices to be made and ritual cleansing to be performed. I don't know how much the seeker would have seen of the aged priestess, the Pythia, and her preparations for the rite. But in the dark secret inner fastnesses of the temple she would sit in a golden chair, possibly breathing in intoxicating fumes from the depths of the earth – the temple is sited on the crossing point of two faultlines – go into a trance, and spew out nonsense which a priest , waiting behind a curtain, would conveniently interpret.

The very last message from the Oracle was delivered to the Emperor Julian the Apostate in the 4th century AD:

> *Tell ye the king the carven hall is fallen in decay*
> *Apollo has no chapel left, no prophesying bay.*
> *No talking spring; the stream is dry that had so much to say.*

The stream is dry, the Pythia is long dead and the temple is fallen – but the Oracle of Delphi, even veiled in silvery mists and rain, is still one of the most magical places I've ever been to.

I need a poem to Apollo to celebrate it, but that will have to wait till we get back to London.

October 18th

The rain is back and drives relentlessly down. We're on our way to the airport and home, but en route, we visit Sounion, with the great temple to Poseidon. Obviously we've really offended him today. It's – you can just about tell through the rain– a beautiful rocky headland, with what should be an amazing view. And it's a magical place, and a sad one; it was from here that King Aegeus, seeing the black sails returning from Crete, thought his son was dead, and threw himself into the sea.

Byron came here just before he went to Athens, and carved his name on one of the columns. Only we don't get to see it, as none of us wants to sit in an aeroplane with wet clothes. So we watch from a café and are served expensive coffee by surly waiters. The café menu, though , quotes the last verse from Byron's famous poem. I hope his Samian wine was nicer than our Sounion coffee.

From   The Isles of Greece   Lord Byron

Place me on Sunium's marbled steep
Where nothing, save the waves and I,
May hear our mutual murmurs sweep;
There, swan-like, let me sing and die:
A land of slaves shall ne'er be mine –
Dash down yon cup of Samian wine!

October 20th

Back in Wales, amber autumn light, fallen leaves, a shimmer of frost. Our heads are full of Greece, even though Richard's head is also full of the unwelcome gift from one of our fellow passengers (yes, it was you, thank you, S_____ from Australia) of a dose of pneumonia. He's sitting slumped in an armchair watching the recent film *Troy,* which we quite liked, though our daughters scorn it as one of the worst films ever made. The sets are impressive, though, and Brad Pitt makes a convincing Achilles, all that scowling prettiness and petulant rage.

It's always a disappointment to find that there are no longer romantic ruins, only sites with ticket booths and a horde of other tourists. Still, on the other hand, no nineteenth century traveller would have seen half the things we see now, thanks to excavations and discoveries. Greece-in-the-head is still there, but now I know more about it.

I loved Mycenae , those nameless gold-covered kings, partly because so little is known about them and you can spin your own web of stories. Though as we heard a lecturer say recently, we probably know more about them than the Classical Greeks did, who had to fill in the gaps with myths.

And Delphi, of course, though I'd like to see it in the sunlight. I promised myself a poem about Apollo, to celebrate Delphi. In Housman's day, every (public) schoolboy knew the story of Thermopylae, that the Delphi Oracle predicted to King Leonidas that either Sparta must be destroyed, or a Spartan king must die in battle ; every schoolboy knew that once the 300 Spartans found themselves caught in a trap in the narrow pass, they calmly sat down on the rocks wearing their red cloaks, and combed their long hair, to the amazement of the gathering Persians; every schoolboy knew how they fought valiantly to the death over three days, and that later, where their bodies were piled, a monument was erected , saying

> *Go tell the Spartans, thou who passest by*
> *That here, obedient to their laws, we lie.*

Every schoolboy knew, but who would know these stories now? There seem to be two Oracle visits here; first to the Dodona Oracle, which doesn't play ball, and then to the Delphic, which delivers the famous message. I can't find a reference to the Dodona visit in the history books, but I'm sure Housman knew what he was talking about.

The Oracles   A.E. Housman

'Tis mute, the word they went to hear on high Dodona mountain
When winds were in the oakenshaws and all the cauldrons tolled,
And mute's the midland navel-stone beside the singing fountain,
And echoes list to silence now where gods told lies of old.

I took my question to the shrine that has not ceased from speaking,
The heart within, that tells the truth and tells it twice as plain;
And from the cave of oracles I heard the priestess shrieking
That she and I should surely die and never live again.

Oh priestess, what you cry is clear, and sound good sense I think it;
But let the screaming echoes rest, and froth your mouth no more.
'Tis true there's better boose than brine, but he that drowns must drink it;
And oh, my lass, the news is news that mean have heard before.

The King with half the East at heel is marched from lands of morning;
The fighters drink the rivers up, their shafts benight the air.
And he that stands will die for nought, and home there's no returning.
The Spartans on the sea-wet rock sat down and combed their hair.

October 21st

Today is Trafalgar Day, and my birthday. But from now onwards I'm in denial about my birthdays, so I shall celebrate Coleridge's instead, which also falls today.

How impossible he must have been as a friend and family member. But what an intelligence ; it shines through even in his darkest days of self-pity and self-abuse. Now he's dead, we don't have to struggle with that conflicted personality.

Frost at Midnight   Samuel Taylor Coleridge

The frost performs its secret ministry,
Unhelped by any wind. The owlet's cry
Came loud – and hark, again! loud as before.
The inmates of my cottage, all at rest,
Have left me to that solitude, which suits
Abstruser musings: save that at my side
My cradled infant slumbers peacefully.
'Tis calm indeed! so calm, that it disturbs
And vexes meditation with its strange
And extreme silentness. Sea, hill , and wood,
This populous village! Sea, and hill, and wood,
With all the numberless goings-on of life
Inaudible as dreams! The thin blue flame
Lies on my low-burnt fire, and quivers not;
Only that film, which fluttered on the grate,
Still flutters there, the sole unquiet thing.
Methinks, its motion in this hush of nature
Gives it dim sympathies with me who live,
Making it a companionable form,
Whose puny flaps and freaks the idling Spirit
By its own moods interprets, every where
Echo or mirror seeking of itself,
And makes a toy of Thought.

But O! how oft,
How oft, at school, with most believing mind,
Presageful, have I gazed upon the bars,
To watch that fluttering *stranger*! and as oft
With unclosed lids, already had I dreamt
Of my sweet birth-place, and the old church-tower,
Whose bells, the poor man's only music, rang
From morn to evening, all the hot Fair-day,
So sweetly, that they stirred and haunted me
With a wild pleasure, falling on mine ear
Most like articulate sounds of things to come!
So gazed I, till the soothing things I dreamt,
Lulled me to sleep, and sleep prolonged my dreams!
And so I brooded all the following morn,
Awed by the stern preceptor's face, mine eye
Fixed with mock study on my swimming book:
Save if the door half-opened , and I snatched
A hasty glance, and still my heart leaped up,
For still I hoped to see the *stranger's* face,
Townsman, or aunt, or sister more beloved,
My playmate when we both were clothed alike!

Dear Babe, that sleepest cradled by my side,
Whose gentle breathings, heard in this deep calm,
Fill up the interspersed vacancies
And momentary pauses of the thought!
My babe so beautiful! it thrills my heart
With tender gladness, thus to look at thee,

And think that thou shalt learn far other lore,
And in far other scenes! For I was reared
In the great city, pent 'mid cloisters dim,
And saw naught lovely but the sky and stars.
But *thou*, my babe! shalt wander like a breeze
By lakes and sandy shores, beneath the crags
Of ancient mountain, and beneath the clouds,
Which image in their bulk both lakes and shores
And mountain crags: so shalt thou see and hear
The lovely shapes and sounds intelligible
Of that eternal language, which thy God
Utters, who from eternity doth teach
Himself in all, and all things in himself.
Great universal Teacher! he shall mould
Thy spirit, and by giving make it ask.

Therefore all seasons shall be sweet to thee,
Whether the summer clothe the general earth
With greenness, or the redbreast sit and sing
Betwixt the tufts of snow on the bare branch
Of mossy apple-tree, while the nigh thatch
Smokes in the sun-thaw; whether the eave-drops fall
Heard only in the trances of the blast,
Or if the secret ministry of frost
Shall hang them up in silent icicles,
Quietly shining to the quiet Moon.

October 23rd

This poem was suggested to me by Katherine Roberts, whose novel, *I am the Great Horse,* told through the eyes of Alexander the Great's famous horse Bucephalas, I'm reading with great enjoyment at present.

It's really just a puzzle poem, depending on punctuation for sense. But it reads as more than that; it has an incantatory mystery about it; the couplets pile up in a thrilling way. Margaret Atwood cited it as one of the first poems that really made her think about what poetry was capable of . It's anonymous and dates back to the mid-seventeenth century.

I Saw A Peacock   Anon

I saw a Peacock, with a fiery tail,
I saw a Blazing Comet, drop down hail,
I saw a Cloud, with ivy circled round,
I saw a sturdy Oak, creep on the ground,
I saw a Pismire, swallow up a Whale,
I saw a raging Sea, brim ful of Ale,
I saw a Venice Glass, Sixteen foot deep,
I saw a well, full of men's tears that weep,
I saw their eyes, all in a flame of fire,
I saw a house, big as the Moon and higher,
I saw the sun, even in the midst of night,
I saw the man, that saw this wondrous sight.

October 24th

Can I really quote this, so well known it's now a cliché, almost impossible to encounter it for the first time, like Vivaldi's *Spring* or the Mona Lisa?

But I do love it, and it's going through my head this morning.

Actually Rameses the Great, whose statue inspired Shelley, hasn't exactly vanished from history. His corpse, returning recently from America where it'd been examined, was given a royal reception, and thousands flock to remember him at Abu Simbel. But the pointlessness, in rational terms, of so many of the great works of the distant past! All that effort into building pyramids, or preserving royal corpses, all for nothing.

> *Let not a monument give you or me hopes*
> *Since not a pinch of dust remains of Cheops…*
>
> *(Byron – Don Juan)*

So many animals, slaughtered at so many altars; all those complicated cosmogonies, all those punishments and penalties, all those prayers and supplications. All that gold, and all that art, just vanished into the ground, perhaps for ever. All those slave-hours of toil.

And yet so much beauty has come from all the rubbish. If the Egyptians had built nothing but mud-brick houses, we'd know nothing at all about them.

Oh, so what. I love this poem, and it's a wonderful one to declaim from the top of a hill, or when you have the house to yourself.

The name 'Ozymandias' comes from a Greek transliteration of one of Rameses II's names. Shelley and his friend Horace Smith each wrote a sonnet to celebrate the arrival of a great Egyptian statue in the British Museum. You can read Horace Smith's effort on Wikipedia – it demonstrates the difference between a great poem and a merely competent one.

Ozymandias   P.B. Shelley

I met a traveller from an antique land
Who said: Two vast and trunkless legs of stone
Stand in the desert. Near them on the sand
Half sunk, a shatter'd visage lies, whose frown
And wrinkled lip and sneer of cold command
Tell that the author well those passions read
Which yet survive, stamp'd on these lifeless things,
The hand that mock'd them and the heart that fed;
And on the pedestal these words appear;
'My name is Ozymandias, king of kings:
Look on my works, ye Mighty, and despair!'
Nothing beside remains. Round the decay
Of that colossal wreck, boundless and bare,
The lone and level sands stretch far away.

October 31st

Halloween, and a time for the spirits to be sitting up and taking notice. I don't imagine there's anything particularly scary going on in our little churchyard; I can see them all sitting there, in dusty black Sunday best, or shawled and bonneted, gnarled hands, rheumatic limbs, but bright eyed and pink cheeked, gossiping softly.

Seen what they done to that old cottage of yours, Davy? Wouldn't recognise her now.

Who's got the place? Folk from Builth, is it?

From London, they say. Spent thousands.

Well, Duw, Duw. This old wall needs a bit of mending now, don't he?

Here's The Lyke-Wake Dirge. (*Lyke* is an old word for death, *fleet* in the third line means 'house-room') Like the Egyptian *Book of the Dead* this poem offers a kind of road-map for the soul, with the difference that the living person also could learn from it how to equip themselves for the journey before it was too late. With its juddering, insistent refrain, it's an eerie and mysterious poem, set to music by many people, but most effectively by Benjamin Britten.

A Lyke-Wake Dirge   Anon

This ae night, this ae night
   Every night and alle
Fire and fleet and candle lighte
   And Christe receive thye saule

When thou from hence away are paste
   Every night and alle
To Whinny-muir thou comest at laste
   And Christe receive thye saule

If ever thou gavest hosen and shoon
   Every night and alle,

193

Sit thee down and put them on,
And Christe receive thy saule.

If hosen and shoon thou ne'er gavest nane,
Every night and alle
The whinnes shall pricke thee to the bare bane,
And Christe receive thy saule.

From Whinny-muir when thou mayst passe,
Every night and alle,
To Brigg o' Dread thou comest at laste,
And Christe receive thy saule.

From Brigg o' Dread when thou mayest passe,
Every night and alle,
To Purgatory fire thou comest at laste,
And Christe receive thy saule.

If ever thou gavest meat or drink
Every night and alle,
The fire shall never make thee shrinke,
And Christ receive thy saule

If meat or drinke thou never gavest nane,
Every night and alle,
The fire will burn thee to the bare bane,
And Christe receive thy saule.

This ae night, this ae night
 Every night and alle,
Fire and fleet and candle lighte,
 And Christe receive thy saule.

November

November 1ˢᵗ

I'm rather fond of November- I like the misty damp afternoons, with the autumn trees still gold and a cold tang to the air. And I especially like November evenings in the city, with lamplight shimmering and traffic flashing red and silver on wet pavements. It's not until February that I go into winter gloom.

This poem by Thomas Hood seemed to be in every poetry book I read as a child, though I'm having difficulty finding it in any of the books on my shelves now.

Thomas Hood was fond of punning, and his puns can be irritating, but I like the way he plays with November so that the very name becomes a negative.

November   Thomas Hood

No sun – no moon!

No morn – no noon-

No dawn – no dusk – no proper time of day –

No sky – no earthly view

No distance looking blue-

No road – no street- no 't'other side of the way'

No end to any Row-

No indications where the Crescents go –

No top to any steeple –

No recognitions of familiar people –

No courtesies for showing 'em –

No knowing 'em!

No travelling at all – no locomotion-
No inkling of the way – no notion –
No go by land or ocean.
No mail – no post
No news from any foreign coast –
No Park – no Ring – no afternoon gentility –
No company – no nobility –
No warmth, no cheerfulness, no healthful ease –
No comfortable feel in any member –
No shade, no shine, no butterflies, no bees,
No fruits, no flowers, no leaves, no birds,
November!

November 4th

A damp, warm morning, some leaves still on the trees, but most of them now accumulating in a soggy mass on the grass and the paths, waiting to be swept up, which , however, I'm not going to do today.

Another Browning poem has been troubling me. There is so much Browning – and so much of it is simply untouchable – *Red Cotton Nightcap Country* for instance; whoever'd go there? But there are many accessible poems I love – *Childe Roland, My Last Duchess, Porphyria's Lover*. And then, troubling poems like this, where you find yourself thinking, Am I getting this? Is this right?

An interior monologue, a male speaker, sitting with his lover in the Campagna, musing about love, and the wandering thoughts that he can't pin down. Is his love as perfect as he feels it ought to be? Do they, even, really know each other? Is love only a momentary sensation? These are hard issues, and as often in Browning's poetry, seem to scrape against the grain of the expected. And then there's the countryside, an expanse of yellowing grasses and feathery wild fennel, which somehow sets all his thoughts drifting through the air like thistledown on the wind. Probably it isn't meant to be autobiographical; it's set among a number of monologues on the theme of love, and the relationship between men and women, all slightly uneasy, uncertain. And yet, as far as we can tell, he and Elizabeth Barratt were perfectly happy together.

Two in the Campagna   Robert Browning

I
I wonder do you feel today
As I have felt since, hand in hand,
We sat down on the grass to stray
In spirit better through the land,
This morn of Rome and May?

II
For me, I touched a thought, I know,
Has tantalized me many times,
(Like turns of thread the spiders throw
Mocking across our path) for rhymes
To catch at and let go.

III
Help me to hold it! First it left
The yellowing fennel, run to seed
There, branching from the brickwork's cleft,
Some old tomb's ruin: yonder weed
Took up the floating weft,

IV

Where one small orange cup amassed
    Five beetles – blind and green they grope
Among the honey-meal: and last,
    Everywhere on the grassy slope
I traced it. Hold it fast!

V

The champaign with its endless fleece
    Of feathery grasses everywhere!
Silence and passion, joy and peace,
    An everlasting wash of air –
Rome's ghost since her decease.

VI

Such life here, through such lengths of hours,
    Such miracles performed in play,
Such primal naked forms of flowers,
    Such letting nature have her way
While heaven looks from its towers!

VII

How say you? Let us, O my dove,
    Let us be unashamed of soul,
As earth lies bare to heaven above!
    How is it under our control
To love or not to love?

VIII

I would that you were all to me,
    You that are just so much, no more.
Nor yours nor mine, nor slave nor free!
    Where does the fault lie? What the core
O'the wound, since wound must be?

IX

I would I could adopt your will,
    See with your eyes, and set my heart
Beating by yours, and drink my fill
    At your soul's springs, - your part my part
In life, for good and ill.

X

No, I yearn upward, touch you close,
    Then stand away. I kiss your cheek,
Catch your soul's warmth, - I pluck the rose
    And love it more than tongue can speak –
Then the good minute goes.

XI

Already how am I so far
    Out of that minute? Must I go
Still like the thistle-ball, no bar,
    Onward, whenever light winds blow,
Fixed by no friendly star?

XII

Just when I seemed about to learn!
    Where is the thread now? Off again!
The old trick! Only I discern –
    Infinite passion, and the pain
Of finite hearts that yearn.

November 9th

In London, and at the British Library this morning, and I'm drawn to the display of writers' manuscripts. Here's 'Reader, I married him,' in Charlotte Bronte's own neat script, and a scrawled-over note from Wordsworth. From modern writers, there's a J.G.

Ballard typescript positively bristling like a hedgehog with corrections, and a foolscap page of beautiful clear italic handwriting from Angela Carter.

There's something deeply moving in seeing the actual manuscript of a poem, just as the author first saw it, especially a first draft, often scribbled over and corrected as new ideas flood in. I suppose now there'll be fewer and fewer of them as we all go electronic.

I'm especially touched by seeing the first rough draft of Isaac Rosenberg's *Break of Day in the Trenches,* next to a letter to in which he affirms his hope of writing poetry 'on a larger scale' after the war. It's written in pencil on a torn-out scrap from a notebook. You imagine him huddled in a greatcoat, scribbling urgently away, while all around him, in the mud and stink of the trenches, dawn is breaking and men are stirring. I thought that the poem had come to him whole and entire, but later I find that he struggled through several clumsy early drafts before he achieved the beautiful simplicity of the final version. In the pencilled draft in the British Library, he writes of a 'queer uncaring' rat. 'Uncaring' is a perfectly adequate word and most writers would have let it lie — but suddenly, in a stroke, he alters it, and there is the heart-stopping 'sardonic'. And he first has the rat crossing 'the poppy-blooded fields' between the lines. Then he has second thoughts, saves the poppies for later, and replaces them with the eerie calm of 'sleeping green'.

Rosenberg, born in 1890, to an impoverished Jewish family, was a little older than many of the war poets, and never started off with their gung-ho enthusiasm. He was a talented artist as well as a poet. He died right at the end of the war, in April 1918.

Break of Day in the Trenches   Isaac Rosenberg

The darkness crumbles away –
It is the same old druid Time as ever.
Only a live thing leaps my hand –
A queer sardonic rat –
As I pull the parapet's poppy
To stick behind my ear.
Droll rat, they would shoot you if they knew
Your cosmopolitan sympathies
(And God knows what antipathies).
Now you have touched this English hand
You will do the same to a German –
Soon, no doubt, if it be your pleasure
To cross the sleeping green between.
It seems you inwardly grin as you pass
Strong eyes, fine limbs, haughty athletes
Less chanced than you for life,
Bonds to the whims of murder,
Sprawled in the bowels of the earth,
The torn fields of France.
What do you see in our eyes
At the shrieking iron and flame
Hurled through still heavens?
What quaver – what heart aghast?
Poppies whose roots are in man's veins

Drop and are ever dropping:
But mine in my ear is safe,
Just a little white with the dust.

November 10th

Walking through Westminster to Victoria after meeting my daughter, I'm struck by the weird silence and absence of traffic all around. A police helicopter is chugging away in the sky and in the distance I hear shouting, a student demonstration, which I later learn, is just at that moment turning nasty.

In the Tube, I'm pleased to see a poem. I thought the Poetry On the Underground initiative had faded away. It's there for Armistice Day, but it isn't a poem I like. It's short enough to quote, though.

Here Dead we Lie   A.E. Housman

Here dead we lie because we did not choose
    To live and shame the land from which we sprung.
Life, to be sure, is nothing much to lose:
    But young men think it is, and we were young.

Housman of course never fought in the war and lost no dear ones. Hence, I guess, his rather weird and chill detachment. Yes, it's ironic, I see that. But it doesn't work for me.

So I turn instead to this poem – and a surprise. For who is the author but Rudyard Kipling, he of *being a man my son* and taking up the White Man's burden. But he lost an only son, and hence this bitter poem:

A Dead Statesman   Rudyard Kipling.

I could not dig: I dared not rob:
Therefore I lied to please the mob.
Now all my lies are proved untrue
And I must face the men I slew.
What tale shall serve me here among
Mine angry and defrauded young?

November 15th

We went last night to a performance of Fauré's *Requiem* as part of a Remembrance day Service, in a bleak, chill vast local church (you feel quite sorry for the Lord about some of the places where He's obliged to put in an appearance.) But while we're in the church, something mysterious happens. For we go in on an autumn afternoon, and we come out in a winter's night. A chill fog has fallen everywhere, tombstones huddling together in the gloom, iceflakes sparkling dully, the air crackling into frost around us. And it doesn't seem to me that winter's been away for nearly long enough – surely there hasn't been enough sunshine in between? Anyway here it is, and this morning everything's frost-white again.

A memory comes at me from nowhere. I am six years old, sitting at my heavy desk by the window of Miss Sinclair's classroom, laboriously writing out these lines. The sharp end of my pencil has broken – my writing is blunted. The broken tip drags on the paper, I can smell the warm aroma of bread-and-milk, feel the soft woolly dress, see the robin-redbreast's footprints on the snowy windowsill, and gulp down a shudder of cold air, all sensations and senses mixed up together with hallucinatory vividness. It's the first poem I remember going straight into my head and making itself at home there - a little haiku-type burst of sensations.

From *Sing-song* **Christina Rossetti**

Bread and milk for breakfast
And woollen frocks to wear,
And a crumb for robin redbreast
On the cold days of the year.

November 17th

Mist and rain today, and this melancholy poem by Edward Thomas seems appropriate. Is it sleep he's writing about, or death?

Lights Out **Edward Thomas**

I have come to the borders of sleep,
The unfathomable deep
Forest where all must lose
Their way, however straight,
Or winding, soon or late:
They cannot choose.

Many a road and track
That, since the dawn's first crack,
Up to the forest brink,
Deceived the travellers,
Suddenly now blurs,
And in they sink.

Here love ends,
Despair, ambition ends,
All pleasure and all trouble,
Although most sweet or bitter,
Here ends in sleep that is sweeter
Than tasks most noble.

There is not any book
Or face of dearest look
That I would not turn from now
To go into the unknown
I must enter and leave alone
I know not how.

The tall forest towers;
Its cloudy foliage lowers
Ahead, shelf above shelf;
Its silence I hear and obey
That I may lose my way
And myself.

November 18th

Time for a change of mood. Here's Absalom boasting of his own splendour from a play by George Peele, the Elizabethan dramatist. He was one of a crowd of wild young men, Marlowe, Nash, Greene, who inhabited the Suburbs of Sin when Shakespeare was a young man, lived recklessly, wrote prolifically and died young. But he wrote some hair-on-the-back-of-the-neck lines:

Gently dip, but not too deep
For fear thou make the golden beard to weep….

Hot sun, cool fire, tempered with sweet air,
Black shade, fair nurse, shadow my white hair….

From   Absalon   George Peele

First Absalon was by the trumpet's sound
Proclaim'd through Hebron, king of Israel:
And now is set in fair Jerusalem
With complete state and glory of a crown:
Fifty fair footmen by my chariot run,
And to the air whose rupture rings my fame
Where'er I ride, they offer reverence.
Why should not Absalon, that in his face
Carries the final purpose of his God,
That is, to work Him grace in Israel,
Endeavour to achieve with all his strength
The state that most may satisfy His joy,
Keeping His statutes and his covenants pure?
His thunder is entangled in my hair,
And with my beauty is His lightning quenched….

November 23rd

When I was starting to read and buy poetry, 'Georgian' was a dirty word. The most influential anthology of the era, the Penguin *Book of Contemporary Verse* , edited by Kenneth Allott can't find a good word to say about them; 'Fortunately there is no need to describe again the characteristic insipidities of the Georgian poets with their cult of respectability and their pastoral week-end England…' And yet, apart from Eliot, who is somehow in a tradition of his own, and Auden, many of those 'contemporary poets' haven't worn at all well. I don't find myself now going to McNeice, Spender or Day Lewis with much pleasure; their 'modernism' seems a bit tinny and tawdry to me. It's the boring old question of 'relevance' – as though a bad poem about a machine is somehow to be preferred to a good poem about the countryside. Being lumped in with the unfashionable crowd has held back the reputation of Edward Thomas, and obscured that of many others. Of course poetry could never be quite the same after the first World War, but that isn't the fault of the poets who wrote before it.

I found this poem by Charles Sorley in James Reeves's anthology of Georgian Poetry We have a rookery in our field , although local farmers hate rooks, probably with good reason. One of our neighbours phones occasionally to say, 'We'll come round today and shoot those old rooks for you,' and is always surprised when I say, no, no, leave them, I like them. Which I do, although they're rough and tough, the Del Boys of the bird world, I love to see them wheeling homeward at night and settling in the highest trees; there's something mysterious and timeless about that flight, which is summed up in this poem by Charles Sorley, a poet who was to die in the Battle of Loos.

Rooks   Charles Sorley

There where the rusty iron lies,
    The rooks are cawing all the day.
Perhaps no man, until he dies,
    Will understand them, what they say.

The evening makes the sky like clay,
   The slow wind waits for night to rise.
The world is half-content. But they

Still trouble all the trees with cries,
   That know, and cannot put away,
The yearning to the soul that flies
   From day to night, from night to day

November 29th

We come back from London to Wales, and find we're turning into people who need many different words to describe snow: this snow is dry, light, iced into cherry-blossom clumps on the trees, intensely sparkly. And intensely cold. Back home, we turn up the central heating, make soup and decide we must be mad. It is beautiful, though, with the turquoise light and the white lace of branches.

> *The owl for all his feathers was a-cold,*
> *The hare limped trembling through the frozen grass*
> *And silent was the flock in woolly fold...*

I'm haunted by that poor hare every winter, and need to remind myself that it isn't a *real* hare. But I shan't quote Keats today – St Agnes Eve is January, not November.

The school bus didn't make it up the road today, so soon we'll expect to see the children of the village tobogganing, dots of joyful moving colour in all the white.

Here is Wordsworth's wonderful description of childhood skating:

From   **The Prelude Book 1 (1805 version)**
William Wordsworth.

>   And in the frosty season, when the sun
> Was set, and visible for many a mile
> The cottage windows through the twilight blazed,
> I heeded not the summons: happy time
> It was indeed for all of us – to me
> It was a time of rapture! Clear and loud
> The village clock tolled six, - I wheeled about,
> Proud and exulting like an untired horse
> That cares not for its home. All shod with steel,
> We hissed along the polished ice in games
> Confederate, imitative of the chase
> And woodland pleasures, - the resounding horn,
> The pack loud bellowing, and the hunted hare.
> So through the darkness and the cold we flew,
> And not a voice was idle; with the din,
> Meanwhile the precipices rang aloud;
> The leafless trees and every icy crag
> Tinkled like iron; while the distant hills
> Into the tumult sent an alien sound
> Of melancholy not unnoticed, while the stars
> Eastward were sparkling clear, and in the west
> The orange sky of evening died away.

December

December 1st

The first day of the last month of my poetry year, and a weather system from somewhere in mid-Siberia is still sitting over our heads.

Stanzas   John Keats

In drear-nighted December,
Too happy, happy tree,
Thy branches ne'er remember
Their green felicity:
The north cannot undo them
With a sleety whistle through them;
Nor frozen thawings glue them
From budding at the prime.

In drear-nighted December,
Too happy, happy brook,
Thy bubblings ne'er remember
Apollo's summer look;
But with a sweet forgetting,
They stay their crystal fretting
Never, never petting
About the frozen time.

Ah! would 'twere so with many
A gentle girl and boy!

But were there ever any
Writhed not at passed joy?
The feel of not to feel it,
When there is none to heal it
Nor numbed sense to steel it,
Was never said in rhyme.

December 2nd

Enough of 'drear-nighted December' - though we're still effectively snowed in for the fourth day. Reading Keats's letters yesterday, I came across a reference to the poetry of Katherine Philips, the 'Matchless Orinda', which Keats had discovered with great delight –'gladdened in the extreme.'

This reminded me that intermittently during this poetry year, I've been trying to find a copy of a biography of Philips that I know I once had. Vanished books can be a mystery – some get thrown out in Great Oxfam Clearups – something we need to do again soon as we're running out of shelf space. Others can be lent – and very few friends are honourable borrowers of books. Some just maybe get swept up in a pile of rubbish or recycling. But I don't think any of these things happened to my copy of 'The Matchless Orinda', which I treasured.

Katherine Philips was born in London, but at an early age married a Welshman and went to live in Cardigan Town, where she formed a coterie of cultivated and artistic friends. Her husband was a Parliamentarian – she was quietly a Royalist supporter. She had two children, one of whom died, and for whom she wrote a moving elegy. Vaughan was an admirer of her work, which she wrote under the name 'Orinda'. She died in 1664 of smallpox at the age of thirty-four.

The strongest emotions of her life seem to have been elicited by women friends, and I think it's this taint of possible lesbianism which has caused her reputation to be occluded over the years ; plus the usual patronising stuff about 'poetesses' and 'minor'. She isn't a major poet, it's true, but she's a considerable and appealing one, none the less.

Here's one, written to her dear friend Anne Owen, whom she called Lucasia.

To my Excellent Lucasia, on our friendship
Katherine Philips

I did not live until this time
Crown'd my felicity,
When I could say without a crime
I am not thine, but Thee.

This Carcase breath'd and walk'd and slept,
So that the World believ'd
There was a soul the motions kept;
But they were all deceiv'd.

For as a watch by art is wound
To motion, such was mine:
But never had Orinda found
A soul till she found thine;

Which now inspires, cures and supplies,
And guides my darkened breast:
For thou art all that I can prize,
My Joy, my life, my Rest.

No bridegroom's nor crown-conqu'rour's mirth
To mine compar'd can be:

They have but pieces of this Earth
I've all the World in thee.

Then let our flames still light and shine
And no false fear control
As innocent as our design,
Immortal as our soul.

December 8th

We drive back to Wales through the weird frozen Narnia that this country has become, with no sign of any Aslan about to break the icy spell. But our heads are full of the concert that we went to London for – a performance by Andreas Scholl and Philippe Jaroussky, of the songs of Purcell. A strange concept – two counter-tenors, for neither of whom is English a first language, singing these quintessentially English songs – it might not have worked, but it was a triumph.

One of Purcell's contemporaries described him as having 'a peculiar genius to express the energy of English words, whereby he moved the passions of his auditors.' – an astute analysis, I think, and English music had to wait until Britten to find another composer who is so sensitive to, and so respectful, of the language. Scholl, too, as a performer, respects and invigorates the words he sings, although he's not a native English speaker . I was especially struck by his performance of Katherine Philip's (Orinda, again, whose biography by the way I have miraculously found on a forgotten shelf) poem 'Solitude'. It isn't actually a great poem, and wouldn't make it into my poetry diary on its own merits - but the poem, the music, and the singing combine in a magical alchemy, so that each word gleams out jewel-like:

> O Solitude, my sweetest choice!
> Places devoted to the night,
> Remote from tumult and from noise,
> How ye my restless thoughts delight!
> O solitude, my sweetest choice!

Philippe Jaroussky, sang *Fairest Isle* with incomparable sweetness. This song comes from a collaboration of Dryden and Purcell. Dryden, a poetic jack-of-all-trades first wrote his opera *King Arthur* as a satire on the accession of King Charles. But he then shelved it, and a few years later dusted it down and recycled it for William and Mary. The second time around, though , he had the advantage of Purcell's glorious music. It was performed in 1691, and four years later, Purcell was dead, aged only 36. Here's Dryden's poem – if you know the music, it will hover around the words in a golden cloud as you read.

Fairest Isle (from *King Arthur*)   **John Dryden**

Fairest isle, all isles excelling,
Seat of pleasure and of love,
Venus here will choose her dwelling,
And forsake her Cyprian grove.
Cupid from his fav'rite nation
Care and envy will remove;
Jealousy, that poisons passion,
And despair, that dies for love.

Gentle murmurs, sweet complaining,
Sighs that blow the fire of love
Soft repulses, kind disdaining,
Shall be all the pains you prove.
Ev'ry swain shall pay his duty,
Grateful ev'ry nymph shall prove;
And as these excel in beauty,
Those shall be renown'd for love

December 13th

We had the thaw, but it hasn't warmed up at all. The hills have faded to a kind of wet-lettuce green, trampled and tousled, with mud and dead leaves sticking everywhere and to everything. The sky is low and thick and grey. There's been too much weather in my poetry diary – but somehow it's been a very weather-y year. More snow promised . General gloom all round.

And it's the shortest day. Or at least, it was in the seventeenth century, before the Gregorian calendar ; St Lucy's day, who with her eyes on a plate must win any competition for the nastiest bit of Catholic iconography. The northern Protestants do better, with girls wreathed with candles. I hope my daughter Lucy never found out about the eyes-on-a-plate.

I'm not quite sure what everything in the first verse of this poem means, but it seems to describe just such a dull, leaden, cheerless day as this outside my window. And there's something else. He's talking about death; and his wife died at just 32 leaving him to care for four children, and with a small income. The carefree poet who laughingly banished the sun from his bedroom window was about to turn into the dour doctor who wrote 'Sin hath cast a curse upon all the creatures of the world, they are all worse than they were at first.' This is a tormented, desolate poem by a man who feels he has little to live for.

A Nocturnal upon St Lucie's Day, Being the shortest day
John Donne

Tis the yeares midnight, and it is the dayes,
   Lucies, who scarce seaven houres herself unmaskes,
   The Sunne is spent, and now his flasks
   Send forth light squibs, no constant rayes;
      The worlds whole sap is sunke:
The generall balme th'hydroptique earth hath drunk,
Whither, as to the beds-feet, life is shrunke,
Dead and enterr'd; yet all these seeme to laugh,
Compar's with mee, who am their Epitaph.

Study me then, you who shall lovers bee
At the next world, that is, at the next Spring:
    For I am every dead thing,
     In whom love wrought new Alchimie.
      For his art did expresse
A quintessence even from nothingnesse,
From dull privations and leane emptinesse:
He ruin'd mee, and I am re-begot
Of absence, darkness, death; things which are not.

All others, from all things, draw all that's good,
Life, soule, forme, spirit, whence they being have;

I, by loves limbeck , am the grave
Of all, that's nothing. Oft a flood
　　Have wee two wept, and so
Drownd the whole world, us two; oft did we grow
To be two Chaosses, when we did show
Care to ought else; and often absences
Withdrew our soules, and made us carcasses.

But I am by her death, (which word wrongs her)
Of the first nothing, the Elixir grown;
　　Were I a man, that I were one,
　　I needs must know; I should preferre,
　　　If I were any beast,
Some ends, some means: yea plants, yea stones detest ,
And love; All, all some properties invest;
If I an ordinary nothing were,
As shadow, a light, and body must be here.

But I am None; nor will my Sunne renew.
You lovers, for whose sake, the lesser Sunne
　　At this time to the Goat is runne
　　To fetch new lust, and give it you,
　　Enjoy your summer all:
Since she enjoyes her long nights festival,
Let me prepare towards her, and let mee call
This houre her Vigill, and her Eve, since this
Both the yeares, and the dayes deep midnight is.

December 14th

'A star danced and under it was I born,' says Beatrice, and it was a good night for a child to be born for the sky was full of shooting stars (Geminids, this time.) And the poem that keeps coming to mind is this by Donne, in spite of the silly misogyny of its last lines. It feels to me like a very early poem so the last verse is merely the callowness of a young man who's too clever by half; but it's a striking poem, and has that directness and immediacy that we love about Donne. For many of us, I think, it's the first Donne poem that we're aware of.

I wonder if he ever showed it to poor, loyal, overworked Ann.

Song   John Donne

Goe, and catch a falling stare,
Get with child a mandrake root,
Tell me, where all past yeares are,
    Or who cleft the Divils foot,
Teach me to heare Mermaides singing,
    Or to keep off envies stinging,
        And finde
        What winde
Serves to advance an honest minde.

If thou beest borne to strange sights,
    Things invisible to see,
Ride ten thousand daies and nights,
    Till age snow white haires on thee,
Thou, when thou retorn'st, wilt tell mee

All strange wonders that befell thee,
   And sweare
   No where
Lives a woman true, and faire.

If thou findst one, let me know,
  Such a pilgrimage were sweet;
Yet doe not, I would not goe,
  Though at next door wee might meet,
Though shee were true, when you met her,
And last, till you write your letter,
   Yet shee
   Will bee
False, ere I come, to two or three.

Postscript

Something mysterious and magical happens this evening. We go down the hill for a walk to the village at the drab end of the afternoon, through heavy greyness, bare trees and tangled hedges. We see no-body and no car or tractor comes past. We return home through fading light and deep silence, everything grey and chill and motionless; as bleak an evening as you could imagine;

All mankind that haunted nigh
Had sought their household fires.

And then in a clump of bare thorn and holly, a bird is singing its heart out- a summery, rapturous, lyrical melody. We stand and listen entranced, but we can't see it. The sound just goes on and on, a glorious looping of notes. We're transfixed, forgetting the cold and gloom.

And a few moments later, I see a thrush flying out of the tree. We almost never see thrushes, but tonight this one sang to us.

I'm desperate to email Hardy and tell him about it, but he's lying in Westminster Abbey without his heart.

But I can thank him for sending me his darkling thrush this evening.

December 19th

I'd love to stop talking about the weather but today there's no getting away from it, with the whole country muffled under a blanket of snow, roads gridlocked, airports closed, pavements turned to ice-rinks. We're in London today, but stranded even so; people tell of bus journeys that should take twenty minutes taking a couple of hours. The world has closed down, shut its doors, drawn its curtains; today every man is an island.

There's only one poem running through my head, and I fear it's one I won't be able to use, as it's impossible to quote T.S. Eliot. But I can write about it, and it can haunt the page as it's been haunting my mind for these last days. It's *The Journey of the Magi*, the poem Eliot wrote in 1927, the year he converted to Anglo-Catholicism

Eliot has adapted the first lines of the poem from a sermon given by Lancelot Andrewes in 1622 :

It was no summer progress. A cold coming they had of it at this time of the year, just the worst time of the year to take a journey, and specially a long journey. The ways deep, the weather sharp, the days short, the sun farthest off, in solsitio brumali, the very dead of winter…..

Eliot the critic held a theory that the mass of past literature was a kind of plum pudding into which writers could put in their thumbs – not as plagiarism but a kind of imaginative reworking, an artistic linking of past and present. Eliot the poet puts the theory to work in the *Waste Land* where the structure is held together and defined by quotation; but I can't think of another poet who's followed his example. It's disconcerting to know that the very striking beginning of this poem is in fact the work of another author, but while Andrewes' words would have been buried in his sermon, by isolating them, Eliot makes them sing out.

But while Andrewes' sermon speaks of difficulties overcome, in Eliot's poem, the difficulties remain. Even the 'temperate valley' into which the Magi descend holds echoes of the Passion and the Crucifixion, with the three trees on the hill and the men dicing for pieces of silver. He's enigmatic about the sight of the Christ Child – there's no joyful epiphany, but a terse comment: 'satisfactory' We expect him to say more about this miraculous event: but there is no more. We're left to puzzle that out for ourselves. Hard thoughts come to mind.

And it's not until the Mage returns home that he realizes the full impact of what he's seen; the pagan gods no longer work, and Christianity hasn't yet been defined. He is desolate and depressed, longing for Death. For an adult, conversion must be a mixed blessing; for every consolation comes an accompanying doubt to wrestle with. And Eliot's poem inhabits that area of doubt; and we inhabit it with him.

December 23rd

As I'm wrapping last minute Christmas presents, I listen to a programme on Radio Three, poems and readings concerned with listening. This one is paired with a lovely Tallis *Misere*; George Herbert invoking a God who seems inattentive.

Denial   George Herbert

When my devotions could not pierce
    Thy silent eares;
Then was my heart broken, as was my verse:
    My breast was full of fears
       And disorder:

My bent thoughts, like a brittle bow,
    Did flie asunder:

Each took his way: some would to pleasures go
    Some to the warres and thunder
        Of alarms.

As good go any where, they say,
    As to benumme
Both knees and heart, in crying night and day
    Come, come, my God, O come,
        But no hearing.

Therefore my soul lay out of sight,
    Untun'd, unstrung:
My feeble spirit, unable to look right,
    Like a nipt blossom, hung,
        Discontented.

O cheer and tune my heartless breast,
    Deferre no time;
That so thy favours granting my request,
    They and my minde may chime,
        And mend my ryme.

Christmas Eve

As so often, it's Hardy who provides the right poem for the day; a poem about the trusting belief of the child, contrasted with the adult's more realistic perception – yet still with hope - as he recalls an old Christmas Eve superstition.

The Oxen   Thomas Hardy

Christmas Eve and twelve of the clock.
    'Now they are all on their knees,'
An elder said as we sat in a flock
    By the embers in hearthside ease.

We pictured the meek mild creatures where
    They dwelt in their strawy pen,
Nor did it occur to one of us there
    To doubt they were kneeling then.

So fair a fancy few would weave
    In these years! Yet, I feel,
If someone said on Christmas Eve,
    'Come; see the oxen kneel

In the lonely barton by yonder comb
    Our childhood used to know,'
I should go with him in the gloom,
    Hoping it might be so.

Christmas Day

A strange, cold, quiet Christmas morning, the light dull and even, everything still. We hear that our nearest town in Wales had the coldest night temperatures in the country and that our road is still a fall of ice. But we'll miss the sumptuous Christmas lunch we would have been having with friends – the only consolation being that later this morning we go to see our family again, and spend a little more time with our granddaughter, just old enough to be excited by Christmas.

The most beautiful Christmas songs are often the simplest, like this one:

I Sing Of A Maiden   Anon

I sing of a maiden
    That is makeles *(without a mate)*
King of all kings
    To her son she ches. *(chose)*
He came all so still
    There his mother was,
As dew in Aprille
    That falleth on the grass.
He came all so still
    To his mother's bower,
As dew in Aprille
    That falleth on the flower.
He came all so still
    There his mother lay,
As dew in Aprille
    That falleth on the spray.
Mother and maiden
    Was never none but she:
Well may such a lady
    Godes mother be.

Boxing Day

Finally we make the journey back to Wales . The fields of Oxfordshire which were once so red with poppies are white and smooth; the compacted snow has an iridescent sheen, and is lit by a soft apricot glow from the sun. No-one has trodden these fields, except a few animals, the windings and scribblings of whose nocturnal meanderings, normally so secret, are now revealed to everyone. There are plenty of pheasants about, some dead, but mostly alive, tawny and strutting. I don't feel sorry for the dead ones; we were taken over by a pheasant once and he was a nasty bully. He ended up run over, too, but we'd had serious thoughts about doing him in first.

Today's poem comes through Radio Three again- a modern setting, as icy and crystalline as the day – of a seventeenth century song – another product of that prolific and mysterious writer, Anon.

Since First I Saw Your Face   Anon (c 1607)

Since first I saw your face, I resolved to honour and renown ye;

If now I be disdained, I wish my heart had never known ye.

What? I that loved and you that liked, shall we begin to wrangle?

No, no, no, my heart is fast, and cannot disentangle.

If I admire or praise you too much, that fault you may forgive me,

Or if my hands had strayed but a touch, then justly might you leave me.

I asked you leave, you bade me love; is't now a time to chide me?

No, no, no, I'll love you still, what fortune e'er betide me.

The sun, whose beams most glorious are, rejecteth no beholder,

And your sweet beauty past compare made my poor eyes the bolder.

Where beauty moves, and wit delights, and signs of kindness bind me,

There, O there! where'er I go, I'll leave my heart behind me.

December 29th

One good thing about this weather – for this is the season when the Unspeakable pursues the Uneatable – is that many hunts have had to be called off.

Here's Pope writing about wintery hunting and shooting; Augustan verse isn't very popular today, and yet, though the heroic couplet does impose a kind of military forward-march on the verse, it's surprising how delicate and subtle Pope can be within its confines. This extract is full of lovely assonances; 'flutters in blood', 'trace the mazes' and liquid consonants. The last line is so poignant – perhaps it's the placing of that word 'little.'

From   Windsor Forest   Alexander Pope

See! from the brake the whirring pheasant springs,
And mounts exulting on triumphant wings:
Short is his joy; he feels the fiery wound,
Flutters in blood, and panting beats the ground.
Ah! what avail his glossy, varying dyes,
His purple crest, and scarlet-circled eyes,
The vivid green his shining plumes unfold,

His painted wings, and breast that flames with gold?
        Nor yet, when moist Arcturus clouds the sky,
The woods and fields their pleasing toils deny.
To plains with well-breathed beagles we repair,
And trace the mazes of the circling hare
(Beasts urged by us, their fellow-beasts pursue,
And learn of man each other to undo).
With slaught'ring guns th'unwearied fowler roves,
When frosts have whitened all the naked groves;
Where doves in flocks the leafless trees o'ershade,
And lonely woodcocks haunt the wat'ry glade.
He lifts the tube, and levels with his eye:
Straight a short thunder breaks the frozen sky:
Oft, as in airy rings they skim the heath,
The clam'rous lapwings feel the leaden death:
Oft, as the mounting larks their notes prepare,
They fall, and leave their little lives in air.

December 31st

And at last this morning, as we look out of the window on the final
day of the year.….

Thaw   Edward Thomas

Over the land half freckled with snow half-thawed
The speculating rooks at their nests cawed,
And saw from elm-tops, delicate as a flower of grass,
What we below could not see, Winter pass.

Envoie

The year's over,
folded away like a flag.

Don't go back there –
you wouldn't like it.

Too much gone,
Places, faces, whole cities,
misunderstood, forgotten,
or simply mislaid.

Don't go back there;
you wouldn't want the knowledge;
snowy wastes, icy winds –
did you think it would be easier?

But there was much to celebrate,
temples in the moonlight,
words in an ancient tongue,
stars streaking the sky,

and a child's voice, inventing the world
with new words, starting over.

And if you didn't quite kill the dragon,
at least it didn't get you this time.
No, don't go back there:
they wouldn't have you anyway.

Time now to open the gate
And pass on through.

Epilogue

So that was the end of the year, and the end of my journal. With hindsight, I suppose we'll remember 2010 as a quiet, icy year, a year of calm before global storms. 2011 has been very different, a momentous twelvemonth of governments and tyrants falling, of riots and violence, of terrible natural events. I don't imagine we'd have wanted to make our journey to Greece in 2011 – no wonder those underpaid waiters were so bad-tempered. For ourselves, the year has brought the usual ups and downs; but we're both still here.

And I notice with a strange shiver that in 2010, I'd marked down December 14th - that day of shooting stars and the magical visit of our own darkling thrush - as a good day for a baby to be born, and sure enough, exactly a year later on that day, our first grandson Jacob Theo came into the world. A star danced.

I'm glad I undertook this odd quest. I've made new friends , people and poems. I've rediscovered old poems that I'd forgotten were friends. I've rekindled some of that early excitement I knew as a young reader, when all this was new to me. I hope that from now onwards, reading poetry will become part of my daily routine.

But I think that most important of all, I've reminded myself how essential poetry is. A poem does something that nothing else can do; only a poem can quite deliver that sudden intravenous shot of pure emotion, that blast straight to the heart. For a short while, as you read a poem, you become a poet yourself; however tired, jaded, dull you feel, a poem sharpens your wits, brightens your perceptions, startles you into life you didn't know you had. You walk out into the world a poet, for a time , anyway.

I decided to try and share my delight in the discoveries of this year by turning it into a book. There were problems, of course; my journal was simply too long and sprawling. It didn't fall into any convenient publisher's category.

And also many of the poems I'd first chosen were still in copyright. Poets should be paid – they deserve it more than most people for the pleasure they bring. But since I was self-financing, I simply couldn't afford to do this. Nor could I bear to single out a few copyright poems – I wouldn't have been able to make a choice. Easier just to lose them all. All the remaining poets have been dead for the requisite seventy years. They're in no more need of copyright payments.

But copyright can be a strange beast; poems by Emily Dickinson, and many by John Clare, are tangled up in modern disputes. This seems perverse to me; copyright should be there for the writers who'd struggled to create these poems, and their immediate families, not university departments or impersonal estates. Anyway, for good or ill, out they went too. I was sad about this. But somehow this only serves to focus attention more intensely on the poems that remain – and there are marvellous poems here which speak for themselves more eloquently than I ever could.

Index of Poets and Poems

Acknowledgements

Many people, knowingly and unknowingly, have helped me with this project. Barbara Nash and Jemma Smy, Colin Tucker, Belinda Hollyer, Bruce Hunter, Diane D'Amico, Paul Ferris, Katherine Roberts, Marlene Hobsbawm, Elizabeth Baguely, Tony and Sarah Thomas, Michelle Lovric, Katherine Langrish, Mark Farrugia and Caroline Walsh have offered poems or information or advice. I'm more grateful to them than they can realise. Richard Rathbone has offered poems, thoughtful advice, and driven me round some of the locations mentioned here. The Scattered Authors Society has provided inspiration, as they always do. Professor Mary Kinzie has very generously allowed me to use her lovely translation of Rilke's poem on Autumn.

As always, my family, Harriet, Lucy, Matt, Lily and now Jacob, have been an inspiration and delight all the days of every year.

CPSIA information can be obtained at www.ICGtesting.com
Printed in the USA
BVOW012338020512

289320BV00011B/2/P